300 PER HOUR
The price for my freedom

Mathilde Davril

300 PER HOUR
The price for my freedom

Max Milo

Max Milo, Paris, 2023
www.maxmilo.com
ISBN : 978-2-315-01-131-5

The Law

Since April 13, 2016, the "penalization of clients" law is in effect. Prostitution in France is legal and authorized. There is an NAF code 96.09.12: other personal services, hostess services, prostitute services, so that people engaged in this activity can declare themselves and pay taxes. On the other hand, the purchase of prostitutes' services is strictly forbidden, and clients of sex workers are liable to a fine of 1,500 euros and 3,750 euros in the event of a repeat offence. Any form of pimping is punishable, such as helping to post an ad, renting an apartment to a sex worker, matchmaking or being a salaried employee. TDS cannot join together and create a structure or they will be prosecuted for pimping. Only the State reserves the right to be our pimp by forcing us to declare ourselves in order to take a part of our incomes, but without agreeing to give us the same rights as other workers: retirement, social security or non-conviction of our clients.

FOREWORD

Why give your body for free when some want to pay? When we are not looking for love, is it better to have *sex friends* or *sex passes*? This could be the subject of a philosophy exam, couldn't it? I can even go further: when our approach does not aim at love, where is the limit between gallantry and prostitution? Is being invited to a restaurant and spending the night with a man, without loving him, disguised prostitution? Or is it simply good manners to pay a bill and a night's stay in a hotel for a woman, so that she is protected from so-called loose morals? Is buying drinks in a discotheque all night and sleeping with an almost unknown man also a way of monetizing your body? Or is replacing cash with spirits in a cup good manners and protects the lady from being a whore? If we meet someone with the purpose of getting laid and having a nice evening, and the man puts in the forms and means, are we whores? Or is it only a palpable exchange of money that turns the tables? If we marry a man for his status, does being married and having a baby guarantee us honor? Or are we not ultimately our husband's prostitute? In what form does money become problematic in an encounter and what is the limit that should not be crossed? And if there is a limit, and we cross it, what is disturbing? That a woman might want to prostitute herself in the name of her freedom? Because being a prostitute, supposedly, is not being free. And yet, everything in this activity could be synonymous with freedom. Sex, independence, choice, pleasure, desire, enjoyment, money, power. My buddies have often said to me, "You, Mathilde, are not a beauty queen, you are not really beautiful, but you sweat sex."

I give off the pheromones of freedom and that's what these men have detected. But should I feel ashamed and on the bangs of society for deciding that feminism goes further than sharing tasks or equal paychecks? Is it not on the contrary an advance in our rights as women to opt for paid encounters? Our right to own our bodies as we wish? To multiply our conquests if we feel like it, while earning money and turning the tables *on* oppressive patriarchal thinking? Isn't prostitution just a progressive trend that clashes with and challenges the ideals of reactionary protagonists? Is it not just uncomfortable for the world to reveal that your husbands, your brothers, your fathers, all of whom are in good standing, use this type of service, without perversity or violence? And that women, normally constituted, who are your daughters, your sisters, your office colleagues, have decided to use their charms, to no longer be oppressed in a scheme that does not correspond to them? Is this really a humiliating burden or an extremely disturbing proof of intelligence? Because isn't the only thing that really belongs to us, our body?

1. What if it was the solution?

I am Mathilde, who has become Mathilda, *escort*, prostitute, whore, whore, courtesan, TDS[1], it's your choice, I have no problem with that. I am your neighbor, your office colleague, the ordinary young woman that you pass in the street on your way to buy your bread or the one that you see in the aisles of Lidl, in jogging suits and with a high comforter on the left side of the head as if to let you guess that I prefer the madness of difference to the wisdom of a smooth and orderly bun. I could be your sister, your daughter and I am a member of a family that could be yours. I am 28 years old and it is February 2012. Two years ago, I left a man who spent more time weighing me than fucking me, for whom kilos rhymed with libido and a ring on his finger with modeling. At the same time, I took the opportunity to kindly thank my boss who assumed that with my advanced age, I would procreate and who, therefore, never agreed to give me a raise. This feeling of being a lemon that has to give its juice, but not to expel a seed, was not worth a permanent contract or a boyfriend.

---

1. TDS: sex worker.

So I arrived in Lyon from my Burgundy home, with that breath of fresh air that big cities have and that lets you know that anything is possible. That at every street crossing, there is an opportunity to meet new people, to discover new things, that being almost an anonymous expatriate in the middle of this crowd of people in a hurry allows me to evolve in total freedom and lightness.

Since my installation, I have been working as a business development officer for a business and legal newspaper. When I answered the job offer, I had no knowledge of the press, had never worked in an editorial office or worked with journalists. I presented myself with the self-confidence I had acquired from my genetic inheritance, and today I am part of the team, without the editor in chief finding anything wrong with it.

I live with Aurore in a three-room apartment in Villeurbanne, Grandclément sector, managed by the OPAC du Rhône. The tenants have no choice, the social syndic allocates the rooms simply according to gender. In our building, there are apartments for girls, boys, families and drug dealers who act as porters in the entrance hall. With Aurore, at the beginning, everything opposed us. I was her umpteenth roommate, she hated the previous one: "As soon as I saw you, I immediately thought you were a bitch".

A great classic! I've often been confronted with this type of *prejudice*, without really knowing why. Maybe it's my outspokenness or the height of my heels.

She was a pretty blonde with long wavy hair and blue eyes, her face still youthful at 20 years old, in a baba cool look, reserved and studious, her nose plunged in her medical books. It took us an afternoon of cleaning the walls of the common kitchen to get used to each other. Today, we are still different, but there is no jealousy between us or lies. We don't try to be what we are not, we don't judge each other and we don't use each other's flaws to exist.

Since I've been in Lyon, I've had one disillusionment after another in love and stories that don't lead to anything. I have the feeling that dating sites are only for "getting laid". In one click, you fuck. The lovers are there one night, one week, the time to take off my panties. The same pattern repeats itself constantly, promising beginnings, seduction, flattery, short term projects, a movie, a love apple at the chestnut vogue, an invitation to go away for a weekend when the sun will be back, obviously not now, a body to body because we feel like it, and then: "You know, I don't want anything serious, I don't want you to get attached and hurt yourself, I feel you're too invested."

It seems that the imprint of previous generations is so strong that men unconsciously associate fucking, commitment, marriage. I fucked her, I have to run away before I have to marry her. Am I not dirty enough or am I too dirty? If I really looked like an independent and frivolous woman, maybe they wouldn't feel pressure? Or is it my image as a free woman that makes them run away? Constantly questioning yourself with this impression of turning in circles. What's wrong, what's not right? What is the key to a successful and ongoing relationship, whether it is a love or friendship relationship? Where are you, the beautiful smiling stranger that I had imagined meeting in the traboules of old Lyon and who would have shown me around the city without hoping to make me pay for my little ticket? Where are you, miss, who promises me at each zumba class that on Friday night we'll go out in a nice bar? Where are you, you who, no doubt like me,

1. What if it was the solution?

are so often alone? Or already too surrounded to open up to new friendships?

After the wonderment comes the disillusionment, and taming this metropolis turns out to be more difficult than my dreams had imagined. The field of possibilities in two years in Lyon has closed on me. I don't have any childhood friends here, nor any college buddies, I didn't go anyway. Office colleagues rarely become friends. There is Delphine, a model in her spare time and a secretary at the law firm next to the newspaper where I work, but although we have lunch together almost every day, in the evening she goes to her boyfriend. There is also Coralie, whom I met through Delphine and whom I sometimes meet for a drink. But, at 27 years old, she has just resumed her studies and is starting a law course, so the penal code is much more important than parties between girls. Aurore, my roommate, is in her second year of medical school and when we meet in the apartment, it's more often to make her recite her pharmacy than to have fun around a good meal. I'm bored and lonely.

One evening, while watching a report on *escorting*, I had a revelation: what if it was the solution? A way to meet people without ever feeling cheated or scalded. A way to occupy my evenings, to go out for dinner and not to stay at home wondering what I am doing right or wrong. That exploring the world of paid relationships won't lead me to love, although madness, isn't it doing the same thing over and over and expecting a different result? Why not try this adventure? Since men are using me, I might as well return the favor. It may be an extreme way to go, but it doesn't seem more shocking or degrading to me than a simple meeting that would start in the darkness of virtual meanders and that would lead to nothing but sex.

I type "escort Lyon" on Google, a multitude of websites appear: Wannonce, 6annonce, Sexmodel, Planescort. I scroll through the dozens or rather hundreds of ads, all the girls look like they come out of magazines. The photos are provocative, but do not look real, like an excess of Snapchat filters mixed with Photoshop. A description sheet details origin, weight, height, measurements, hair color, shoe size and a small presentation text accompanies it. Some of them are quite crude, listing sexual practices that I don't understand, abbreviations or English words: GFE, *Extra ball*, Creampie, BDSM, *In-call, Facesitting*. To indicate their prices, they speak of roses: thirty minutes, 150 roses; one hour, 250 roses; then the extra, extra sodomy or facial ejaculation. Everything is square, like a product data sheet on Amazon.

Out of curiosity, I click on "registration", on a free site, the interface looks like Meetic's. I create an email address: mathilda.escort@mail.com. Mathilda, I think it sounds good. It's soft, suggestive, feminine, like all these first names ending in A and which without being pronounced refer to the heat of the Mediterranean. Emilia, Ella, Yasmina, Sophia, Guilia, Paola. It only takes one letter for the fantasy to be born. Marcelle is no longer the same woman when she is called Marcella and the men, without even seeing her, already have the feeling of guessing and desiring her.

I select a photo of myself in lingerie, a shot taken to satisfy the voyeuristic appetite of a non-transient lover, and to satisfy my need for flattery in the moment. I am a young woman, far from the standard of the Elite models, but well dressed and adorned

1. What if it was the solution?

with frills that compress the excess and pigeonhole the missing, I find myself pretty and feminine. I don't write any presentation text, nothing comes to my mind except: for sale against good care! I simply note in the box "coordinates" my new e-mail. In a few minutes, my ad is online and I am overwhelmed with messages a few hours later.

"Hello, you look lovely and I would like to meet you, Eric, 59, very sweet."

"Seen on Lovedreams.com, are you available right now to come to Valmy, Lyon 9? Fred, 45 years old."

"Hello, can you tell me what your rates and services are? Charles, 53."

"Hello Mathilda, it is so pleasant to discover your voluptuous photos that invite the pleasures of the senses. A wind of freshness and novelty blows on the site and I would like to swirl at your side. I hope to read you and charm you. Jean-Jacques, 62 years old."

"Hello Mathilda, my name is Vincent, I am 35 years old, athletic, rather good looking, 1m80, French. I'm looking for a special fantasy at home Lyon 1er. I'd like to be masturbated while you force me to sniff your feet, smelly if possible. Can this interest you? With pleasure."

"Available 30 minutes for fellatio, 100 euros ? Medhi"

"Rates and benefits?"

"Hello charming lady, I am on a trip to a 4 star hotel in the Presqu'île. My name is Thierry, 52 years old, normal appearance. I would be delighted to receive you for 2 hours. Can we exchange?"

It's unexpected, I never imagined that I would receive such a quantity of messages in a few moments. The men want to meet, they leave me a little description of themselves, of their desires and sometimes attach a photo. I don't answer, I simply read the mails and sometimes I am stunned by the crazy requests, even though, for the majority, the fantasies expressed are not extravagant, and few of them go into the details of the sexual service. But considering prostitution is one thing, getting past it is much more difficult. I don't have the courage for this first meeting, nor do I have the poise to respond to a courteous and charming e-mail. I am torn between good and evil, between my Judeo-Christian background and my thirst for adrenaline mixed with my need for freedom. I find myself ridiculous to want to monetize my body, just because my daily life is platonic and full of disillusionment. But I want to live differently, not to undergo anymore, but to be an actress of my life as a woman. I didn't leave everything behind two years ago to let myself be locked into an existence that doesn't resemble me. So, maybe yes, for once, I could be free to make my own choices and prostitute myself if I wanted to, without feeling all the pressure of society telling me that I don't have the right to do so and that this would make me a woman who doesn't respect herself.

2. MY GIRLFRIENDS ARE DOING EXTRAS

- What do we order, Coralie?

- A glass of champagne and a board to nibble on. Is that okay with you, Mathilde?

I'm on the terrace of the K, a trendy bar-club in the chic district of Brotteaux. The heated mushrooms bring warmth in this evening of March 2012. Although she is busy with her new studies, my friend has taken her head out of the penal code for once. Coralie is not one of these women on whom one turns around in the street, it is her charm which makes her beauty, this coldness which freezes some or which makes others want to warm her up. She is neither pleasant nor sympathetic, she gives herself the air of a narrow middle-class woman that one cannot approach. But she is whole and frank when she breaks her shell, which has made us become friends for a few months. Life has taught me not to stop at *preconceptions.*

- Coco, I want to tell you about something I'm considering doing, but I'm a little afraid of shocking you.

- Shock me, though, that's strong, I'm not that uptight! What do you want to do that could be shocking? You can talk to me about anything, don't worry.

- I'm going to get straight to the point, I signed up on a site. An *escorting* site. I haven't met anyone yet, but I posted an ad. I'm thinking about experimenting with this type of dating, but I can't seem to get started. I'm afraid, but I don't know of what.

- It's funny that you should talk to me about this, I wasn't expecting it. But I'll put you at ease, I understand you perfectly, I've been doing *escorting* for some time now.

I am stunned and I find myself shocked, as if caught in my own trap. She who pretends to be a scared little virgin is actually an *escort* ? She that we want to call "Madam", in her chic suit and with her mannered looks? I finally meet few girls in Lyon, what was the probability that one was a prostitute? Is it really more common than I imagine? Is it just a coincidence? I never suspected that she could have this type of activity. It's true that she wears a luxury bag, has had a nose job at the Clinique du Parc, has just returned to school at the age of 27 and doesn't work on the side. But it is not obvious as a connection, and she does not correspond to the image that one makes of a girl of joy: she is neither vulgar nor lost, I never saw her taking drugs, she seems happy, fulfilled and never evoked to have undergone abuses. This is a very simplistic vision, but it is the one that is mediated when we talk about the profiles of prostitutes.

- Coco, you play me? Do not say anything! You, you are an *escort*? Attention, do not see in my astonishment a form of insult, but admit that your announcement is unexpected.

- I'm an amazing young woman, and you know, it's not as complicated as it sounds. You have to be careful, you have to select the clients. If you want, I'll explain how it works and help you get started. To start, you must have a professional phone and register on the 6annonce site, it is the best. On the others, the clientele is shitty and it's 100 balls an hour. This one is paying for girls, 150 euros per month, normally it's 300, but I have a special link to pay less from France. Anyway, it pays off quickly and it's quite simple to set up. It's actually a very common hobby. I shouldn't tell you, you have to keep it a secret, but Delphine is not really a model! She works for an agency in Geneva, in Switzerland it's legal. On the other hand, you are not independent. The owner sends you on a mission when a client selects you and you have nothing to say.

I get a second electric shock. Delphine? The young woman I have lunch with every day? The one who every morning, before entering the law office, goes through the newspaper shouting on the doorstep of my office: "Come on Math', good luck for your morning", in a laughing tone, like a comedian who has found the joke of the century and who never gets tired of it. And who, in the evening, says to me as full of life as ever: "See you Math', I'm off to school! I'm going home to my darling, tonight it's spaghetti!

This Delphine? All wise and all cute from the top of her meter seventy-five, her perfect curves and her skin so deliciously golden that she overshadows the Eiffel Tower when it is glittering? This Delphine who never knew how to explain to me why she associated a party in the air to a plate of pasta?

- Is it the tangling and twisting? Is it because it's long and thin?

- No, it's because spaghetti is pretty!

I have been seeing her daily for almost two years! Am I so gullible? What is this hidden world, which apparently has a large number of followers? Could it be that it is actually very common? These girls have a seemingly ordinary life, job, studies, boyfriend, apartment, social life.

- Coco, why are you doing this?

- Because I'm single and I prefer to get paid rather than to be taken by men. For the money too, and for the freedom that this way of life brings. Thanks to this, I can resume my studies without being in a precarious situation. I offer myself a new future and I find it pleasant to be a seductress, because it is not necessary to believe that all the men treat the *escorts* like merchandise. That's not true, I'm more often a marriage counselor than a blow-up doll. Not everything is glittery, but if you set yourself a code of conduct, then you minimize the risk of bad encounters.

These revelations give me the impetus and the courage that I lack. Sharing this with Coralie becomes simple, it is no longer a solitary journey into an unknown world. I am an initiate and I have a testimony, not through a trashy report of *Exclusive Investigation*, but face to face, with a young woman that I know and who now gives herself up without reserve. On her side, she was initiated by a girl who had herself been initiated by another. She tells me that there are many young women who are involved in the business as a result of an unpremeditated meeting or opportunity, and who then evolve in the shadows and without any suspicion, because a conventional social status allows them to sow doubt.

I follow his advice, buy a prepaid phone and redo an ad on the Internet. I apply myself, elaborate a nice text of presentation which praises my human qualities, my altruism, my frivolity and I add some photos, blurred face and tattoos. I delete my profile on Adopteunmec.com, validate my registration on 6annonce and don't feel that there is much difference between these two sites. The objective is to meet people, to reach carnal pleasures, for one by making his future partner dream, for the other by paying her.

In mid-March 2012, as soon as my ad was published, my cell phone kept ringing. The market in the prostitution sector is unimaginable when we are not directly confronted with it. I am not talking about ten calls per day, but about fifty. And on this Internet site, which by some means escapes the regulations against pimping, we pay to be listed and can display our rates. Mine, as a beginner, is 250 euros per hour. About fifty men try to contact me every day, ready to pay 250 euros to have a sex party with a professional, which I am not, of course. Nevertheless, I have always been good with people and with the telephone, and when I was younger I worked as a teleprospector. I sold slimming cures and wine. So, when you are capable of getting someone to buy a case of vintage wine at 1,000 euros, without them having tasted it, simply by the force of a well-practised sales pitch and a smooth voice, it's easy to sell yourself. All you have to do is to establish a speech, to be smiling, dynamic and the interlocutor is hooked.

My first exchanges are hesitant and shy. I don't know what the expectations and demands of these men are, nor what I am able to offer them. Talking about sex with your partner is not easy, so with a stranger it is destabilizing.

At the beginning, I familiarize myself with the vocabulary of the profession and orient myself on a niche, that of the GFE, in English *Girl Friend Experience*, i.e. the role of the girlfriend. I don't propose any extreme practices or scenarios, nothing I don't like, no domination and even less submission. I kiss, but I don't swallow, I sell my ass, but I don't have it penetrated. Paying to have sex as ordinary as with your wife, there is a clientele for that, and that is the one I am interested in.

My biggest problem is the age of the gentlemen who contact me. Most of them are 50+, I'm not 30 and have little experience. I'm not a scared young virgin, I live my sexuality as a single boy of my generation would allow himself to do. But I am not ready to take the step of a mature man, not for my first time as an *escort*, I need to start this game on familiar ground.

3. A PRICE THAT MAKES ME A PROSTITUTE

It's 12:27 p.m. on Thursday, March 15, 2012, when I take the call, at the newspaper, between two forks of my mixed salad, almost laying on my computer keyboard. I swallow my mouthful, and with a natural, relaxed air, I launch into this vocal exercise I've been practicing for the past few days.

- Yes, hello?

- Hello Mathilda, my name is Jérémy, I am 35 years old. I'm calling about your ad, are you available tonight?

Tonight is perfect, it doesn't give me too much time to think and I have enough work at the newspaper to keep my mind occupied. I'm not afraid that something bad might happen to me, that I might get hit, raped or drugged. The anxiety I try to alleviate by burying my head in my files is similar to the stage fright one feels at a job interview or when the curtains open on a performance night.

I leave the office at 5 pm, without having completed any of my tasks. Finally, I worked without working, I thought without thinking about anything, I rambled. I take the C3 bus back home, it is crowded and the traffic is heavy at this time of the day.

The trip lasts about 30 minutes, I feel like I'm out of my body. There are dozens of people around me, but I don't see anyone, don't hear anything despite the hubbub of the crowd in public transport. I am like in a bubble. A bubble of stress mixed with excitement. My heart is beating fast, I have palpitations, sweaty hands and red cheeks. I could pass out, right now, on the floor of the bus, but it arrives at my stop, place Grandclément, I have to get off.

I make a detour to Carrefour before going home, buy a bottle of white wine and put it in the freezer while I shower. I take my time, shave my legs, wash my hair carefully. On my way out, the towel still wet around my body, I pour myself a glass. The bottle is not very fresh, it doesn't matter, I pour myself a second one, light a cigarette, then another one. I do an impeccable blow-dry, I am almost platinum blonde and my length falls to the shoulders. I opt for an evening make-up, a *smoky-eyes* a little too pressed. I put on a pair of stockings, a pretty black tanga and a *push-up* bra. I choose a dress in the same color, short, but flared not to mark my hips and my thighs too fat. I tighten it with a belt to emphasize my waist which is rather thin. To finish my outfit, I put on a pair of twelve centimeters pumps. I observe myself in front of the mirror in my small room of ten square meters, I find myself pretty, even if I am not sure of myself and a little shaky. I have curves and do not correspond to the standards of the profession. I reassure myself that he has seen my pictures and knows that I am not skinny. It's silly, I care if he likes me. Could he say to me as he opens the door, "No, go home, you're too ugly."

Does this kind of thing happen? Surely. And that's what scares me the most right now.

I pour myself a last glass in the kitchen and meet my roommate Aurore.

- Where are you going all dolled up on a Thursday night?

- I go out to dinner with Coralie.

- You're beautiful, are you sure it's Coco you're going out to dinner with?

- It is not safe to meet the prince charming! If you want a glass, the wine is cool, I'm going.

- Give her a kiss for me and take care of yourself.

The few sips of wine have calmed the palpitations of my heart. I get into my car and, during the forty-minute drive, I smoke one cigarette after another. I ask myself what I'm doing: "This is crazy, it's nonsense, it's probably dangerous, you realize, you're going to be a whore anyway, it's not nothing." I dial Coralie's number to share my emotions with her and get the support of this knowledgeable woman.

- Hello, Mathilde, are you on your way? How are you feeling? Anyway, it's not your first date or your first time!

- I feel like a young virgin! I'm hot, I'm excited and at the same time I'm a little scared.

- It's normal, and you'd be in the same state if you'd met this guy on the Internet without the pricey side. Just tell yourself that you're going to meet someone new. I also have a date tonight, he's coming by my place in thirty minutes. Call me back if anything goes wrong or to tell me when you're on your way home.

I arrive in this small town outside of Lyon, disconcerted by what I am about to do. I park my car in the parking lot of the condominium. There is not a living soul, not a sound and the night is plunged in the most complete darkness.

3. A price that makes me a prostitute

I take a strong mint gum from my purse and spray myself with *Coco Mademoiselle* so I don't smell like a cigarette. During the few steps I have to take to get to Jeremy's house, the echo of my heels echoes in my head, I feel as if I'm dizzy by myself, unless it's the white wine I drank as fast as a Perrier on a hot day? I take a deep breath, fix a commercial smile on my face, I am in front of the door. What will happen, what will it look like? I'm full of adrenaline. I have the rubber band around my ankles, I'm on the edge of the bridge facing the void, I jump: knock-knock.

The young man opens the door with a wide smile and a look that sweeps me, almost scans me. I am immediately struck by his athletic appearance, he is not very tall, dark, his face is square, smooth, youthful. He is very drawn, structured, as if made. He must not count his hours lifting iron in the gym or plucking his eyebrows. He has a physique halfway between a bodybuilder and a rugby player. He's not what I pictured. To me, if a boy pays, he must be ugly, fat and probably a little disgusting, otherwise he wouldn't need to pay. Why use an *escort* when certainly half the girls in the gym want to spend an evening with him? I am pleasantly surprised and the pressure of the whole day starts to come down. For the first time I put a face on a client of the prostitutes and I find this young man as ordinary as all the others I meet on my way to the office. He could be my bank advisor, my salesman at Decathlon or the HR guy who recruited me at the newspaper. At first glance, I don't see anything in him that differentiates him from an honest man.

His apartment is coquettish, without pretention. He welcomes me in a small, pleasant and neat living room, just like him. A flat screen is hung on the wall and a video game console is underneath. Some green plants decorate the room and in a corner a Tancarville on which underpants and tee-shirts spread carefully are drying.

He invites me to take a seat on the sofa bed next to the wall of the room just behind, it is plunged in the dark. I try to be at ease and to get to know him naturally, but my nervousness has taken over my aplomb. I don't know how to lead this dance I'm discovering. Can I ask him personal questions? Is this done? Or should we hide from each other? Who is more illegal? We are adults and consenting, but can we disassociate? Can I reveal myself to him? Should I put my hand on his thigh when he talks to me? Should I make the first move? At what point should I make the move? What are the habits and customs of this profession? I don't have the instructions for prostitution and there is no such thing *as* Escorting *for Dummies*! I realize that Coralie taught me the technique, but did not teach me anything about the practice.

I feel Jeremy is a little tense, not very friendly. I am like him, only worse, but if we forget the envelope he gave me at the beginning of the meeting, we are like two young people trying to tame each other during a first date. He doesn't suspect that this is my first experience of *escorting,* and I don't question him about what pushes him to use this service. Your baker never questions you:

- But finally, why do you come to buy my bread?

- It's true that it doesn't look well done, I'll go elsewhere, thanks!

He offers me a whisky and even if I don't like it, the pure malt soothes the palpitations of my heart, the effect of the white wine vanished at the same time as my realization on the parking lot. The verbal exchange between us doesn't last very long, he didn't offer himself this extra time to elaborate. He sweeps up the

3. A price that makes me a prostitute

subject of sport, lifestyle, but doesn't reveal anything personal, and I don't ask him any questions. I remain distant so as not to be intrusive. We have to hide, the less you know, the better, the less you say, the less problems you will have.

He quickly leads me into the room. His pleasant physique plays in my favor. I sleep with him, as one is deflowered by a man whom one does not really like and whose time will erase the memories. A blow job, a cunni, a doggy style. No spanking or hair pulling, no raw words either. Just an act, without embellishment nor madness, without flavor as much for him as for me. A first time without thrills or disgust, similar to a thousand first times in real life. With one difference, I left less than an hour later, with the envelope containing the 250 euros in my purse, the price that now makes me a prostitute.

- How did the first meeting go?

- Why is the guy paying? He was good looking, nice, clean and he didn't even look stupid. In an hour's time, the only complaint I have about him is that he's not the hit of the century!

- They rarely are! My client tonight was not either! However, he was a doctor. We expect them to know our bodies perfectly, but I believe that feminine subtlety cannot be learned from books.

- If he is a general practitioner, he must be confronted more often with infected throats than with wet pussies! Gynaecologists should be tested!

- Never done! I imagine that when they get off work, they want to see everything except a girl without panties! And how do you feel ?

- Less poor! I'm 28 years old and even though I have many years of relationship behind me, I've long since broken the statistics of the number of partners in a woman's life! It was similar to a romp with a guy who would have made me dream just to get undressed. But tonight, I'm not going to question why he doesn't call me back!

I go home just feeling like I spent the evening with a young man, not a client. We've burned a few bridges and probably will never see each other again, but is that so different from my single life? And I don't feel dirty or soiled, I don't scrub myself in the shower any more than usual and I don't have a conflict with my self-esteem. An envelope doesn't make me any less respectable than I was that morning, nor does it make me a poor victim of men.

4. Paying is not cheating

- Lunch at Terreaux Math' ? There's a new salad bar! Mathilde, why are you looking at me like that?

If Coralie hadn't given me this heavy secret to keep, I would have shared my new adventures with Delphine. But how to broach the subject without forcing her to reveal herself? I don't want her to lie to me, I prefer that she doesn't tell me all her truths.

- Sorry Delphine, I was in my thoughts. Did your *shoot* yesterday go well?

- Yes, as usual!

- It's for a poster campaign, right? When is it coming out?

- Oh! I don't know, there is never a fixed date.

The judgment of others, the fear of misunderstanding, and the fear of being seen as fools who can't do anything better than sell their asses force young women to hide. It is not easy to break away from an image devastated by an industry fraught with criticism and censorship. However, after my first appointment as an *escort*, this mode of meeting seems obvious to me. The requests and desires of the men are not frightening. They contact me politely, without vulgarity, sometimes appearing shy and with no other wish than to live a moment in mutual respect. I don't choose my partners on photos like on a classic site, but I select them carefully. It is enough for a man to be on first-name terms without my agreement for me to end our telephone conversation, or for him to send me too many messages before our meeting for me to cancel it. If he changes his first name and age with every text message, I don't respond. I have a history of all the conversations. They probably delete them so they don't leave evidence and don't remember their cover, but I keep everything. When I refuse an appointment, I systematically record the number under the name "Blacklist". An intonation of voice, a practice I don't like, a spelling mistake, I am intolerant and never give men a second chance. But some people find it difficult to accept that I can be selective:

"Who do you think you are? You're just a big shitty whore, I'm going to fuck up your ad, put comments on you, you dirty whore".

"French shit, we know where you live, we're going to find you, I'm going to come with my friends, we're going to rape you, you deserve nothing but this, you French bitch. You think you're a woman, you're just a bitch, bitch."

Not all men are courteous and charming in this environment, but I never respond to attacks and obnoxious messages. Giving importance to these types of personalities would only accentuate their grotesque fantasies of domination. And if I hadn't been vigilant and demanding, I probably would have had problems with them.

Meeting a mature man does not seem any more insurmountable than meeting a man in his thirties. I'm discovering that mature men have that extra touch of delicacy that young men don't have. They are wrinkled, but elegant, courteous and respectful. I don't ask for more. I limit myself to active and athletic 50-year-olds, to men who on paper do not scare my lack of experience.

- Hello beautiful lady, my name is François. I am 53 years old, slim and toned. I would like to meet you. I can welcome you at my hotel in Lyon Part-Dieu for two or three hours this Tuesday, starting at 7:30 pm. We could get to know each other while enjoying some sushi and a nice bottle of white wine. If you are interested, I can send you a photograph. Let me know your wishes and possible taboos. I wish you a nice evening, François.

- Hello François. Thank you for your very nice message. I can make myself available this Tuesday. I suggest that we exchange by phone, it will be nicer. I work by *feeling* and simplicity. Call me according to your availability. Kind regards, Mathilda.

I accept this appointment, because when a man offers me a dinner or an aperitif, I know that I am not a commodity, that my host does not order me only to satisfy his primitive needs. He expects a warm atmosphere, in which the game of seduction and the discovery of the other are more important. I don't appreciate receiving a photo, I prefer blind encounters, but men often tell me their height and weight even if I never take the initiative of this question. I don't care about looks, and if a man is elegant, well-groomed, respectful, then he becomes charming. My lovers have never been beauty canons. I like to read a story on a face, not to admire a drawing.

I joined François in an apartment hotel on Avenue Berthelot, in the 8th district of Lyon. Before taking possession of the room, we get acquainted around a Perrier slice on the terrace of the

4. Paying is not cheating

hotel bar, at the bottom of a small green inner courtyard without other customers to come and disturb our confidential meeting.

- François, what are you doing in our beautiful city of Lyon?

- I am here several days a week, I am a judge. I live in Bordeaux, but for the moment I don't have a position in my region. I hope soon to stop traveling and get my transfer.

In the room, we talk about the peculiarities of his profession, even the lawmen break it, and about his personal life. His wife has been suffering from cancer for several years and is now living in a nursing home. That's why he allows himself this kind of extra, to escape from a daily life that has become too heavy and from a heavy solitude. Loneliness is a word that comes up regularly when I meet people or when they ask for help.

- But you, Mathilda, are not made for this life. You don't belong in this environment. I don't know you very well, but you have a certain aura about you. You have a quick wit, your eyes are bright and sparkling. What is your story, what led you to this kind of meetings? You don't have to answer me.

Yet, it is because my eyes are bright and shiny that *escorting* is for me. As crazy as it may sound, I am happy to be here tonight. To discover this man, to listen to him, to tell him my story without cheating and without acting, because after my first experience, I decided to be myself during my meetings and to allow myself to live these meetings as naturally as when the men do not pay me. We share the sushi platter at Matsuri's, I tell him my story and feel his desire rise with every bite and word I say. I allow him to put his hand on my thigh when he approaches me to fill my glass of Saint-Véran, then I give him the permission to unbutton my blouse and let him go down delicately to my femininity. Because, contrary to what we imagine, during these meetings, I am the one who dictates the behavior and sets the rules. The men do not allow themselves what they want, but do what I allow them.

Accepting appointments gives me the feeling of being alive, of existing, of no longer being the one who undergoes, but who blossoms in an art and in a new way of apprehending life. I am no longer isolated or confined in my metro-business-sleep pattern. I go out, meet interesting people who value me, elevate me intellectually and allow me to reach a social rank that was previously unknown to me. I meet executives, business leaders, artists and politicians. My job at the newspaper allows me to have a knowledge of the economic fabric of Lyon and the country, so I shine in front of them during our meetings, by exposing them my few notions acquired from reading the weekly newspapers. For the first time, I feel glorified by men who don't try to manipulate me. When there is no obligation of result, there is no lie. The attention and interest they show me is sincere and devoid of pressure related to a form of commitment. We exchange with great honesty about our respective lives and our daily lives.

During the day, when I'm at my desk at the newspaper, I close my office door, take calls and answer messages. At the gym, which I attend much more regularly to shape my new work tool, my phone is next to me. And so is Coralie, because from now on we never leave each other's side, this activity forges a real complicity between us. I realize that she does not spend much time on the university benches and her penal code seems to me too dusty to be regularly leafed through. We go to sports together, we meet before or after our appointments, sometimes she even

4. Paying is not cheating

accompanies me for an afternoon at my parents' house or meets me at the roommate's.

- Where are you going out again tonight, Mathilde?

- I find Coralie.

- You don't leave her side! Sports, parties, are you in love?

- Aurore, stop your nonsense. It's just that I like her, she's my friend.

- I still find all your outings a bit strange.

- If you didn't have ten more years of schooling ahead of you, I'm sure you'd come and have fun with us.

It is impossible for me to tell Aurore the truth, for her to check every night if I am back, for her to worry about me and for my choice to become a burden for her and a hindrance in her studies. I don't want her mind to be disturbed by a life that doesn't belong to her. I know that this is not what you want for your friend, your daughter or your sister. The business I'm in doesn't get a lot of press and there are a lot of concerns about this business. The violence, the drugs, the *hardcore* sex, the unknown are scary. When we think of prostitution, we imagine the Bois de Boulogne, the violent clients with their big bellies and filthy clothes, the girls who suck for 20 bucks to be able to shoot up, and the pimps who come to strip them after having beaten them up and forced them to sell themselves. This is very far from my reality, even if it also exists. And as a fervent defender of freedom, this face of prostitution scandalizes me. It is a profession that one must practice of one's own free will and that requires maturity and reflection. You can't become a prostitute at 16 and discover your sexuality through this. At the age when we dream of love, sex with a stranger has no place. In this innocent period of self-discovery and discovery of the other, paid encounters have no place. And it is not insignificant to be detached from one's body, from the other's physique, to perform a sexual act, when we teach little girls from a very young age that sex cannot be dissociated from love, that sleeping on the first night is being a slut and that having more than five partners in the course of one's life is being a whore.

I am fully aware that minors incited by unscrupulous men find themselves in the turmoil of this activity. That women who are promised a better future are forced to work under pain of various reprisals! It is this aspect of prostitution that most of us know. The one that the media talks about and that is used to establish the laws that govern this sector of activity. We take the worst of it, we make it a generalization and we say that for the good of all, we must repress, contain, prohibit and abolish.

For centuries, according to my Wikipedia research, France has not known how to deal with prostitution. In 1254, prostitutes were chased out of the cities by the royalty, all their goods were seized and the pimps had to pay a fine. Two years later, the same king, Louis IX, reversed this ban and invited prostitutes to practice, but in a hidden way and outside the cities. Three years later, prostitution was once again illegal. Two hundred years later, the regulation not being registered in the codes of the revolutionary laws, the activity is again decriminalized. One step yes, one step no! In 1800, the girls were considered as vectors of disease, they were forced to register and had to make monthly medical visits, but the activity was not reprehensible. In 1945, Marthe Richard, forced at the age of 16 in the 1900's to perform 50 passes a day in brothels for soldiers and who became a city councilor in the 4th district of Paris, after marrying a rich client, introduced a bill to close brothels. The majority of the establishments and the owners being closely involved in the collaboration during the war, the law is validated four months later. General punishment. End of the ball! It was probably easier to close down brothels than to sue those responsible for allowing the enemy to have fun.

Fifty years later, in 2003, before his mandate as president, Nicolas Sarkozy, then minister, had the parliament adopt the "law for internal security" which included passive solicitation as a new criminal offence:

"The fact of publicly soliciting another person by any means, including a passive attitude, with a view to inciting him or her to sexual relations in exchange for payment is punishable by two months' imprisonment and a fine of 3,750 euros."

This law aiming at abolishing street prostitution only creates additional stress for women living from this activity. And for those who work under pressure and coercion from a pimp, in addition to their low remuneration, there is this possible fine and prison sentence. In other words, it plunges the girls into misery, but neither protects them nor helps them, and does not make the prostitutes and their clients disappear. Nothing will ever make this activity disappear, as long as sex exists. There will always be lonely, dissatisfied men, who want to taste another body or who don't want to be burdened with feelings or commitment. And there will always be women like me who think that the heart is much more precious than the body. Because in this type of dating where adultery is often the focus, it's not about love or deception. Paying is not cheating. It is much more indelicate and much more dangerous according to men to have a mistress. I will never be intrusive in their personal lives, no texting in the middle of a family weekend or blackmailing them into love. With me, they have no pressure. They have the advantages of adulterous relationships without the disadvantages. And getting paid is not the same as accepting everything. For me, I have all the good aspects of the first love, all the precious moments of the beginning. Every time I meet someone new, it is the promise of a first time, of the game of seduction, of flattery, of small gifts, of a glass of champagne in a subdued atmosphere, of a romantic scene in the fabrics of comfortable beds in luxurious hotel rooms. And just like them, I don't expect anything, I don't hope, I am the mistress, but I don't suffer it.

A man once said to me, "You know, Mathilda, if I didn't allow myself these little extras, I wouldn't be with my wife anymore, and yet I adore her, she is the woman of my life."

The fidelity of body does not have anyway really its place in the real life. It's a fantasy that humans nourish. Can we really spend twenty years of our life with someone without feeling desire for another person? Are we capable of never succumbing? Can we spend decades longing for our partner? Routine, daily life, children, the passing of time are all ingredients that encourage weariness in a couple. There are those who assume their desire for another skin and who act on it. Those who make love with another person in mind. Those that only the lack of opportunity holds them back and makes them faithful. Those who are not interested in sex. And that small category of beings who are stronger than the majority of us, for whom one plus one equals one, without ever weakening.

A man accepts her infidelities without any problem, he pays for it and to avoid trouble, but he wants a natural meeting, with an ordinary girl who does not make him feel with every blink of an eye that he paid to meet her.

"I'm looking for a casual, low-dating girl, have you seen anyone this week yet?"

"How long have you been practicing, do you have a side business or are you just doing this?"

"Don't come dressed in a vulgar way, I like elegance and refinement in a woman."

These questions and requests are my daily routine. They want an *escort* who, preferably, does not work. They order a whore, but if I really am one, I become less desirable, less attractive. And I don't do this business like I thought I would before I was confronted with it. I never enter a hotel room without a smile on my face, undressing directly and undergoing for an hour the perverse fantasies or not of a man who has no respect for me. This is not what they expect, the cerebral side has more weight, seduction is paramount. The femininity, the charm and the exoticism of a forbidden relationship increase the excitement tenfold and make sex almost secondary, almost accessory.

5. Funny fantasies

At the beginning of April 2012, I met Olivier on a Saturday night, at the Novotel de Gerland in the 7th district of Lyon. A wrestling match is being played just across the street, at the Halle Tony Garnier. We had an appointment for the second half of the evening. He put an envelope with my name against the champagne bucket and serves me a glass when I arrive. He is a smiling and relaxed 40-year-old, he is part of the organization of the event and takes a little break. The atmosphere between us is friendly, wrestling is an atypical sport that I know little about. He confirms me that everything is rigged, that the games are done in advance, but that the show is beautiful, original and full of testosterone. It is a classic meeting, an ordinary man that one could have as friend or husband in life. After a few flutes, we start a physical approach, kisses, caresses, basic foreplay almost boring, then he asks me to come and sit on him. I straddle him for a few minutes when, "Could you pee on me?"

I know that the uro, the scato are practices that exist. Practices that are beyond me, among others, I don't know what pleasures we can take from it. Is it related to humiliation, to the need for submission? It seems that men with power like to be reframed. A spanking, a dildo belt, it channels them and makes them stronger in society.

"Piss on me, spit on me, I'm a piece of shit and fuck me. Whip me by the way and insult me."

I have a hard time imagining that one can come out of it valued, but I can conceive it without judging it too much. I can't stand cutting my spaghetti, it's my Italian side, but everyone does what they want on their plate. Here, it's the same thing, everyone does what they want in their bed.

I've already received requests like this by SMS:

"Would you like to sit on my face for an hour? I lick you and you piss on me, I drink it all."

Strange fantasies, personally I prefer the St. Joseph.

Regularly, a man writes to me:

"Could you come and tie me up naked to my bed and leave so my wife can find me like this?"

It's special. Although I would like to see what happens next. Does this staging turn the lady on? Does a hot fuck come out of it? Or does Madame, frigid, take offense at finding Bernard tied to the bars of the bed?

"If you weren't so uptight, I would fuck you! Untie me Elizabeth, I'm going to take you wildly! Let the sex demons take you over! I want you!"

But since I don't have the end of the film, I don't answer the *casting of* the second role. Everyone has their fantasies, as long as all parties agree. But I don't enter into any delusion or scenario of a stranger, I prefer to stick to what I know how to do, what I master, which doesn't force me to perform acts that I don't like, even if I think that we can have sexual deviances without being *serial killers*. Besides, I use the term "deviances", but where does normality lie?

There, I am confronted in the middle of the action with an unusual request for service. The man wants me to urinate on him! It's not that bad. For the average person it's just disgusting, but I can't do like I do with a text message, not answering it, I'm still on him. I have to interact and I have to weigh my words. I don't want him to get offended and react aggressively. I am always vulnerable to a man, so I control my behavior even if he is not threatening. He is just waiting for an answer, if I say yes he will be delighted, if I say no he will be disappointed. But I prefer to play dumb, it's more reasonable and less brutal.

- It's a little dirty, isn't it? There's going to be a lot on the bed, a lot on the sheets. We're in a hotel room, it's a little tricky for the cleaning lady, don't you think?

From the taco to the tac, he answers me:

- No! Not if you aim right.

He is lying on his back. I'm still standing over him. I think in my heart: "No, incredible! He's daring too!"

- If I aim well? That is, if I aim well where?

- In my mouth.

He said this to me in the same tone as if he were offering to take a climbing class next week. I wasn't expecting that at all. My speech and my announcement cannot be confused. He knows that if I don't agree to a facial ejaculation, I'm not going to urinate in his mouth. But I find it comical and a bit cheeky. He's putting me in front of a fait accompli, he has the guts to do it. It's not a sudden urge on his part, it's premeditated. Even though he never brings it up in our conversations, I know for a fact that he had this little idea in mind. I can't believe it was an instant thing: "Here, how about I make myself a little pee digestif for a change."

By telling me about it before our appointment, he would have faced a no. By putting me up against the wall, he can get a yes. And he's right to try, on paper, I'm here to fulfill men's fantasies.

- In your mouth? I don't really feel like it. Besides, I don't have to pee.

- Too bad, I would have liked that. You want some more champagne, it will give you...

- I'm good, thanks. Let's do some doggy style instead, what do you think?

Our coitus and our appointment end in a conventional and relaxed way. We do not return on this parenthesis. I do not try to know what attracts him in this practice. I regret it while leaving, I would have liked to satisfy my curiosity, because I am not very much confronted with exuberances. Apart from this atypical case, all encounters are similar and so are all men.

The typical profile is 50 years old. He is on a trip to Lyon, is an executive or a company director. Married, he is bored alone in this city that welcomes him for a few days. During his first evening, he scours the *escort* websites and plans an entertaining little party to break the solitude of his nights away from the marital home. He receives me in a suit and has taken care to bring up a bottle of champagne before my arrival. He put on a jazz *playlist* and put on perfume. He is used to this kind of meetings, he offers himself this pleasure three or four times a year. He wants seduction, stockings, suspenders, fresh flesh and languid foreplay. Nothing extravagant, to be sucked other than with the tip of the lips already fulfills him. Don't think that they perform with me more than with their wives. I even tend to think that it's worse. When we know that the average duration of a sexual intercourse is 5 minutes and 40 seconds, with a new skin, some fine lace frills and the forbidden aspect of the thing, the time is often divided by two. I add to this that two thirds of these tiny minutes of lovemaking are devoted to cunnilingus. So I have neither the time necessary to reach orgasm nor the time necessary to get sore or even sweaty. The vision of the prostitute being fucked wildly for the whole hour is pure fantasy. Let's not overestimate these gentlemen! Because even if I refer to this famous survey carried out on five hundred couples during four weeks, the results go from 33 seconds to 44 minutes, it would still miss sixteen for the phantasmagorical vision of our art to become reality.

6. Rich news

The room in my flat share costs me 280 euros of rent per month. I have a car credit, a budget for cigarettes, outings, clothes, classic expenses. I earn about 1300 euros net per month at the newspaper, a salary which is said to be "correct", but which is more objectively miserable. I'm not in debt, I'm in balance with a reasonable lifestyle and desires that match my low income. What initially was not a source of motivation for me, money, quickly became an obsession. Feeling all that cash is exhilarating, enjoyable, I never had a euro in my pocket before. I now pay for my bread with a 50 euro bill. A feeling of power, of power and especially of freedom invades me with each new envelope that a man gives me. I set up a ritual that gives me immense pleasure, I count and recount the small denominations hidden in kraft envelopes between my mattress and my bed base. I am like a child, receiving two 50 euro bills disappoints me, having five 20 euro bills amazes me. When I started *escorting,* I had 500 euros in savings. I come from a modest family, the end of the month always started on the 10th. A few weeks after my first appointment, at the end of April 2012, I celebrate my birthday on the white sandy beaches in Punta Cana. Massage every morning at the club's spa, boat trips, diving in the lagoon, pina colada until I couldn't drink anymore, rum parties with the other vacationers, souvenir shopping for the family, the girlfriends. Ten days of dream, without counting, I could never afford this before.

"Money does not make happiness, but happiness does not fill the plate"[2].

The carefree nature of a life without restrictions, it is easier to accommodate excess than deprivation and I quickly acquire a taste for doing and buying what I want, without thinking.

When I return to the newspaper, I find in the bottom of a dusty drawer a small beige iron box, like the one used by shopkeepers to store cash, before electronic machines. I commandeer it and bring it home to give it a second life. With small hair elastics, which are usually used to finish a braid, I make bundles that I hide preciously in the box under my bed. Now I'm going home from my official work by cab. At 5 pm, public transport is crowded and 20 euros do not put a strain on my finances. I no longer spend 100 euros on shopping, but 1,000. I no longer buy Sephora, my make-up remover is now Dior, my handbag is leather from Lancel and my sunglasses are gold from Vuitton. I don't go to the rue de la République anymore, I shop on the rue du Président Édouard Herriot, always with Coralie. Our canteen is a Paul Bocuse brasserie and my favorite salad is the one with lobster. I no longer look at prices when shopping, I no longer compare the cost of one brand to another, I simply buy what I want and what I enjoy.

---

2. Booba, *Little girl.*

- Do you have plans for tonight, Aurore?

- I'm going to review.

- It's Friday, don't you want to get some fresh air? Come and have dinner with Coco and me, I promise we won't be back late.

- That's nice, but I don't have much money...

- That's not the point, forget about the money, I'm inviting you.

- You're already paying for everything for me these days.

- I don't pay, I invest! When you're a cosmetic surgeon, you'll give me free lipo!

- I will never be a plastic surgeon, I want to be an anesthesiologist.

- You still have time to change your mind!

- But where do you get your money from, did you win the lottery?

- It's just dinner! I didn't ask you to rent a private jet to eat margherita in Sicily!

I wish I had, because my taste for luxury is something I pick up very quickly. Like a new rich person some might say, or rather like an old poor person. When we can't afford it, we settle for what we can afford. We are satisfied with a new dress from H&M at 19 €90 and we find ridiculous the women who put 2000 euros in a handbag. We pretend, we lie to ourselves. Because most of us are affected by this consumerism syndrome. When you've always lived overdrawn and on the 10th of the month you don't have a euro left, if you triple your salary, if an inheritance adds six figures to your bank account or if the lottery makes you a millionaire, you buy. You love fishing? You'll invest in the most efficient reel. Are you passionate about sewing? Build a haberdashery in your living room. You love nature and camping makes you feel free? Then you hit the trails with the best hiking boots and the most ergonomic tent available. For the first few months, you allow yourself to do things you've never been able to do before. That's human, and I'm human.

Money makes me beautiful, strong and gives me an impression of omnipotence and a feeling of exacerbated freedom.

I now walk the carpets of Lyon's palaces, Louboutin shoes on my feet, head raised and determined gaze. No address holds any secrets for me anymore: Villa Florentine, Hilton, Cour des Loges, Carlton. I no longer admire an inaccessible world through a window, it has become my daily life. I am no longer afraid to enter a luxury boutique, just to look, because I can and do buy, because for my prestigious clients, I must be an elegant young woman, wear a silky dress over lacy panties, and shape my image and body.

I have always been obsessed with my extra pounds. When I was 20 years old, I weighed 74 kilos for 1m63. My jeans were size 42-44. I went on my first diet at 16 and I've done them all, high protein, low calorie, Weight Watchers, Slim Fast, Dukan, cabbage soup. The anxiety of the scale, the daily weighing, and yet, since I was a little girl, I have had a healthy diet, no soda at home, few sweets, fresh vegetables, but I was born with the overweight gene. I wear size 40 when I start to play with my charms. I'm lucky to have a rather slim waist and a tummy without bulges, but my stockings are bouncing around in my saddlebags and my cellulite-filled buttocks, although bouncy, are soft as a marshmallow. I have never been a great sportswoman. I was one of those who tried to get an exemption at school. As I was the chubbiest in the class, my classmates didn't want to train with me. It was quite traumatic, I must admit. I don't know if the teachers have changed their work methods since then, but I can still see myself at school in this gym that looked like an execution center. All lined up, Mr. Robert, our teacher, would choose two team captains. Then, each in turn, in front of the whole class still lined up, my classmates designated the members of their group. The more the vise tightened on me, the more :

- Go ahead, take Mathilde.

- No, you take her. I don't want her, she's too fat, she can't run.

- Come on, you already have Nicolas, he's the strongest, so take the weakest.

- No, I don't want that fat cow on my team, she's useless.

To avoid this humiliation, forgetting my things or getting a prescription saved me from this affront. Kids are mean, no question about it! But fortunately, in my day, there were no social networks or opportunities for harassment outside of school like there are nowadays, or I could have made the front page of tragic news stories.

Today, I do a lot of training in the gym, but you can't get a goddess body in a few sessions. I ride my elliptical bike for miles and offer myself Cellu M6 treatments. I want to be beautiful, thin, the one I never was. I work naked and have always had a complex about it, it's paradoxical. I sell a body that I don't like to men who pay to have access to feminine curves, which only exist on glossy paper.

One evening, I was invited to Alexandre's home, quai Claude Bernard, on the left bank of the Rhône in the 7th district of Lyon. I get ready, taking care to be attractive, and go to the address indicated, with this confidence that from now on will never leave me. The man opens the door for me, he is a young man in

6. Rich news

his thirties with a bourgeois look and a style of dress that often distinguishes "daddy's boys", the Ralph Lauren shirt and the little sweater tied on the shoulders. He stares at me and undresses me with his eyes from head to toe: "You're not my type, I like thin, beautiful women. I don't pay for that."

And he slams the door in my face. I am disconcerted and offended. What I had feared had finally happened. He didn't take the slightest bit of care, he didn't have any humanity towards me. In his eyes, I am just a commodity that does not meet his expectations. Why be delicate? I am not a real woman or a real person. I am "it", a product that must meet a precise specification.

I keep this fact to myself, I am too ashamed to talk about it to Coralie. But I don't let myself be destroyed by this bad encounter, which is only the reflection of a generation where appearances are more respectable than know-how.

7. Two is better

My debut in the world of sex work made me realize that it is not incompatible with a so-called normal life, and I don't feel any more different than any other girl. I go to the office every morning, *looking a* bit better than before and not choosing between appetizer or dessert at lunch. But other than that, nothing has changed in the way I feel about myself. Trading my body doesn't make me bitter or resentful, and the men I'm with aren't violent predators.

- You know, Mathilde, in this world, we get the customers we deserve. It's a bit brutal, but I mean it. I have never had a mishap, because I don't accept everything for money. I don't offer half an hour or an appointment only for a blow job. I select only the requests of high quality services. I always talk on the phone to get a feel for the person, and that's why I don't deal with clients who could hurt me. When you accept everything and anything, you expose yourself to what goes with it.

- Speaking of high-end services, I thought of something, Coralie, to practice differently, to reach new men and make more money by working less.

- Isn't it a slogan, work less to earn more?

- Almost! But I reworked it! It was for Sarko's presidential election, but he said: "Work more to earn more". Which, in my opinion, is completely stupid. Working less to earn more, that's a concept that becomes interesting!

- That's right, and what is your concept?

- I suggest you make a duo offer, I'm sure it can be a hit. Men all fantasize about doing two girls at once. We keep our respective ads and make a joint one.

- I thought about it, but I wasn't sure you'd be up for it, you're still in your trial period in this business! But, how are we going to work less and earn more?

- We will offer this service at a higher price than our usual hourly rate. This is a service that must be paid for. 700 € for the package, that is to say 40 % of increase each.

- Do you think guys are willing to spend 700 bucks an hour to get two girls?

- It is possible to try.

- What about working less?

- There are two of us, we share the task over an hour and what makes men fantasize is to look at the girls.

- But neither you nor I are bi.

- Yes, and there's no way I'm licking you! However, there are subterfuges for faking and hiding. What do you think?

- I'm pretty convinced, even though you didn't invent much!

We do a common photo session in lingerie. We take the break in profile, back, play with the light to intensify his brown and my blond. The result is enticing, even captivating. We publish our ad during May 2012:

"Mia & Mathilda, why choose when you can have both? You dreamed about it? We did it! The sensual blonde and the sultry brunette get together for more delights. Come and experience our infernal duo and let's triple the pleasure together."

Coralie, unlike me who lives in a shared apartment, receives men at her home. Her building is secured, she gives the address in front of her windows and, when she considers that the person is in conformity with her expectations, she gives him the right address. Receiving at home allows us to enlarge our clientele, to reach a public that does not wish to pay for a hotel room in addition to the service. We offer our services *in-call* and *out-call*, as we say in our jargon, i.e. on the road and at Coralie's home. As I imagined, we have calls, we are not overwhelmed by solicitations, but our ad attracts curiosity and interest.

Philippe was immediately seduced by our duo, and he called me on the first day of its publication. I was in the office when I spoke to him mid-morning, and when I said into the phone :

- We don't do anal...

The door to my office opens. As usual, the director of the newspaper comes to take place on the chair in front of me, with his broad smile full of suspicion. I feel the red in my cheeks and lower my eyes to regain control of my emotions.

- I'll call you back later, Mom.

- I get it, you can't talk anymore, call me back when you're free.

- Well then, Mathilde, a big girl as you still call her mother?

- You know, Mr. Béthod, we are always our parents' children, no matter how old we are!

- So, did she get hurt?

- No, why is that?

- I thought I heard, mind you I wasn't listening, but I heard something like, "Bad, we're getting hurt or not hurt."

- You are not listening, but you are very curious! I said, "We do no harm!"

I'm sure he understood the meaning of my sentence perfectly, but as an elegant man, he doesn't bully me for long and goes on with the life of the newspaper.

The next day, I went to Coralie's house after leaving the office and having taken care in the morning to prepare a small bag with a change of clothes. The day before, the meeting was scheduled with Philippe, he is our first partner.

- Are you okay, Coralie, you're not too stressed?

- No, it's okay, we should be fine!

I am in a little black dress and stockings, I always keep this feminine accessory during the meeting to avoid skin to skin, and the nylon shapes the thighs, attenuates the orange skin and camouflages if the depilation is not perfectly clean. Coralie is in a nightie, bare legs. I don't think it's very classy, it's even vulgar to receive guests in nightwear, it doesn't leave any room for imagination and it's too much in the thick of things, but she's at home and she's used to dressing that way.

The doorbell rings, the palpitations of my heart are no longer felt, even for this new first time.

- Hello Philippe, Mia, nice to meet you.

- Hello Philippe, Mathilda, nice to meet you.

We greet each other in the most classical way, by kissing each other.

- Come on in, we're going to the living room. Would you like something to drink? A coke, a coffee, a glass of water?

- Yes Mia, with pleasure, a coke please.

I take the envelope while Coralie in the kitchen serves us something to quench our thirst. Philippe is in his fifties, 1m80, 90 kilos, with a three days beard, an ordinary physique, clean, neither handsome nor ugly, with a little bit of weight.

The three of us are sitting on the couch, him between us. It's a strange situation, but I proceed as usual, I'm friendly, smiling, creating a bond and taking an interest in the man who comes to enjoy himself with us. I hide the main objective, my only goal is to relax the atmosphere and to make this moment as natural as possible. Philippe tells us that he is in the digital business, that he has sold solutions to Google and created several applications. He remains a bit mysterious, but does not hide the fact that he is the subject of reports. We sip our drink while talking, me leading the way, Coralie being in the background. Some girls do not appreciate the exchanges, it is the case of my friend, she prefers to dispatch the service and is little interested in the men whom she meets. Me, I need the human side to occult the tariffed aspect. From time to time, Philippe puts his hands on our thighs and compliments us.

- You girls are really pretty, it's a delight to have you by my side.

He comes closer to me to kiss me, then turns to Coralie to give her a kiss. We invite him in the room, bathed by the half-light of the shutters almost entirely closed, the bed is covered with a sheet carefully installed for the occasion, and we take place all three on it like lovers who would find themselves thus every Thursday afternoon.

I've never had an experience with more than one person or with another woman. I have kissed on the lips of girlfriends at parties that were a little too festive and duly drunk. Alcohol disinhibits and exalts feelings, a smack becomes a proof of unconditional friendship. But I never embraced my tongue to a woman's, never found myself naked to caress her and to plunge my head between her thighs. Coralie and I haven't agreed on anything, haven't established a plan or a way to proceed. It's like jumping into the void without having anticipated a safety net.

Philippe is lying on his back between us two. He kisses us in turn by letting himself undressed by our four hands. We caress him by delivering kisses on each side of his neck while going down slowly along his hairy chest.

- Take off your clothes and kiss each other, I want to look at you, you are so sensual.

The fateful moment is here. It's not a dreaded moment, it's just a first time.

Coralie and I stand up. We are always on each side of him and advance our busts to embrace us and mix our languages above his amazed eyes. Coco and I play this scene without any emotion, but we don't let anything show to our partner who touches our bodies simultaneously, not hiding his excitement. What he does to one, he does to the other.

I remove the nightie of Coralie by delivering her soft cinematographic kisses and by letting her unbutton the buttons of my dress. We are now naked breasts and overhang Philippe who rises to come to lick our naked breasts. In a dash of greed, he attracts me against him and seizes my mouth, by rocking us both against his body of again lengthened. We slip up to his tended sex and begin a fellatio with two mouths and four hands. One sucking his penis and the other one increasing tenfold the pleasure by putting her lips on his hot and wet balls. Philippe moans, serves the sheet between his fingers and asks me to sit on his face. I am now spectator of the scene which plays in this apartment in the heart of the Part-Dieu. We do not exchange any glance with Coralie, we know our respective roles and know what we have to do. I push small cries to satisfy and reward Philippe who seems to enjoy my vagina. He invites Coralie to take my place, we exchange our positions. But the foreplay can last very long if we do not put an end to it. I take a condom on the bedside table and while Philippe delivers a cunnilingus to my colleague, I dress his glans with latex and come on him. Instantly, I hear him moan while having the mouth full of Coralie. Philippe is on the verge of orgasm and invites us to get on all fours. We are both tense rump and remind him that he must change condom at each change of partner. He makes some comings and goings in each one of us, before withdrawing his condom and pouring his semen on our offered buttocks in front of him.

- This is a new experience to check off the bucket list!

- Mathilde, was it really in your list?

- No, but with two guys, yes! Where do you think I got the idea for the duets?!

- Have you never done it?

- No, I'm too much of a prude!

Philippe came back the following week and a few more times. We also meet other men, some of whom take us to dinner in the city's fancy restaurants. Two elegant young women sitting with a man, does the waiter make the connection or does the picture look so big that we look like nieces or secretaries?

We also participate in festive evenings during company seminars to entertain executives of large groups. We have to put on a show, dance on the tables, dine without panties and designate the best "pussy eater" of the executive committee. The president, stopwatch in hand, gives 20 seconds to each participant of the contest, the winner gets the panties as a trophy! You have to be uninhibited and playful, which Coralie is less and less.

- I remind you that I have to study Mathilde, I do not intend to be an *escort* all my life. You, if you are happy, so much the better, I am better than that.

- Study Coralie, you're right. It would be a shame for you to become what you already are, if you think you're better than you are. And I don't feel like I'm "it".

I put her derogatory remarks down to pressure, to life, and I can perfectly conceive that she might be dreaming of a different future. I turn a blind eye to her mood swings and her sometimes hurtful attacks.

8. What is the problem?

In May 2012, two months after I started *escorting*, my sister Marina, 18 months my senior, gave birth to her first child. And even though we had a perfectly similar upbringing, we are on opposite ends of the spectrum. My sister is one of those women with a well-ordered life, without hindrance, to whom everything succeeds socially. The ones who are involved in associations, bake homemade cakes for birthdays and organize Saturday afternoon Thermomix meetings. She is a citizen and a model daughter. She pays her taxes without trying to cheat, never exceeds the speed limit and always gives way to pedestrians. She doesn't smoke, they say there's a time for everything and when you're an adult, THC is no longer required and neither is nicotine. I don't know who decreed rules for different ages or when we become adults, but the guy must not have been much *fun*.

At the beginning of her career, she followed the same path as our father and became a truck driver before training again as a saddlery-maroquinier for a large French luxury house. One of the most important criteria for hiring is the ability to represent oneself. My sister has a sunny personality, it must be genetic because the women in my family are all like that. She inspires and attracts sympathy despite her serious air and apparent rigor. She has had less than five lovers in her youth and her greatest folly, after playing hooky and shooting a few rounds of firecrackers as a teenager, was divorcing her first husband and marrying her current husband, a law enforcement official, with whom she gave birth to her first child the year she turned 30. As much as to say that there is no place for the offences within its hearth.

I love driving at 130 on the ring road and overtaking on the right. I smoke, regularly drive with an alcohol level higher than the authorized limit, cannot count the number of my lovers, am only manual when it comes to rolling joints and refute any form of authority, wisdom and commitment. Speed, adrenaline, party, I'm always *borderline*. Our commonalities stop at the fact that we have the same parents. We never make identical children, my mother will tell you, although we do try to give them a similar education. No doubt one grew up and the other did not!

But our difference in life has never kept us apart. Several times, after a family meal, when there are only two of us left at the table, a little tipsy, I feel like telling him about my appointments. But it's like admitting to someone that you've cheated on them, it eases your conscience, but hurts the other person. Maybe she can hear and understand it, but confessing to her big sister who cherishes and idealizes you as much as you idolize her: "I'm a prostitute", it stains the family record book. Even if current events could be used as a springboard to discuss the subject with my loved ones, I don't have the strength. As for Aurore, I fear that they might worry about me.

Najat Vallaud-Belkacem, having made her mark in the political fabric of Lyon, has decided in recent weeks to surf on the subject of prostitutes. Carried by her new functions of Minister of Women's Rights under the Hollande presidency in the summer of 2012, she seizes our way of life and screeches in the media: "My objective is to see prostitution disappear".

Minister of Women's Rights, it's a great title, but should we know and understand women, all women. Because talking about rights when you want to reach our freedoms, isn't it contradictory? This is not the Ministry of Women's Rights, but of some women. And if we are less hypocritical, we could even rename this ministry: The Woman Must.

Roselyne Bachelot, Minister of Health, one year earlier declared: "There is no such thing as free, chosen or consented prostitution."

These two politicians, who have certainly never been in contact with prostitutes in their lives, make themselves our spokespersons, without being interested in our milieu, the different aspects of our profession and what we would like. They stigmatize us in the same way as veiled women. It can't be our doing and we can't find fulfillment. I don't consider myself a victim and the men I meet are not my executioners, despite the well-meaning society, which tries to put a shameful pressure on me. There is a free, chosen and consented prostitution, even if in all cases something motivates us: money, freedom, sex, independence. We all have a different vision of this activity and, as with all subjects, nobody has a universal thought.

To the question:

- But what if you didn't need the money?

I answer:

- And you, would you go to the office in the morning?

À :

- Isn't it degrading to sell your body?

- Isn't it more painful to offer yourself to a man who seduces you and doesn't call you back?

À :

- If you had to do another job?

- I would choose a job where I can be free, where being a woman does not affect my rate of pay and where I would not be disadvantaged compared to a man, but rather glorified by him.

And to :

- But being a commodity for men is not glorifying and prostitution is not a libertarian act.

- I am no more a commodity than you are to your boss.

Glorified, because when a man pays you several hundreds of euros to be with you, that he writes to you to know if you are well returned, invites you again, because he appreciated the last moment in your company, puts the small dishes in the large ones, that sometimes he cooks for you and offers you flowers, there is only degrading the image that one makes of it.

Because, in reality, what is it that bothers you about paid relationships? The number of lovers? The money, said to be easy, which is linked to it? The exploitation of the body? But doesn't a model or an actress use her body? You will tell me that there is no sex. So that's what's disturbing, sex? But isn't sex life? Certainly, I do not give it. But do you only have sex to give birth? No, but you will answer me: "I only have intimate moments with my lover, my husband". So, finally, it is the number of my lovers that bothers me? No, it's the fact that you get paid. So it's the money that's the problem? But do you and your partner always split the bill 50/50? Do you always put the same amount in your joint account at the beginning of the month? For the apartment he bought before he met you, and in which you are now living, did he charge you an entrance fee to balance the monthly credit payments he has already made? When he buys you gifts or flowers, does he bring you the bill so that you reciprocate in a perfectly fair way? Or is it that, finally, as he earns more than you, as is often the case in French households, he puts more money in his pocket? So, after an evening at the restaurant, where he invited you, and you make love on the way home, can we somehow say that you got paid? I hear you retort: "That has nothing to do with it, he is my husband and I love him". So, are feelings the real problem? But, should I be incriminated because I am single and I live as I want?

Because a man who pays me does not delude me, but treats me and respects me like a woman he would like to have. I am unattainable and that is what makes me attractive to him. I am that courtesan that he cannot possess. I have power over him. He buys my body, but mostly my time, fantasizing about being able to afford my heart, my desire and my pleasure. You could probably tell me that in "real life", we also meet beautiful people. Certainly. But my experience is that the men who pay me appreciate me much more than those who don't: "Thank you very much, Mathilda, for this unforgettable moment. I know it's utopian, but I want to propose to you. I am capable of leaving everything for you and you would be the happiest of women by my side. Your Florent".

8. What is the problem?

Humans like to possess what seems inaccessible to them, and this is what makes me precious in their eyes during these paid encounters.

9. Living for the better

Two years ago, in 2010, doctors diagnosed my dad with a severe form of prostate cancer, the year he turned 52. They gave him only a few months to live. With treatment and radiation, he was cured, but then he developed lung cancer and then peritoneal cancer. Now he lives with an ostomy pouch and the metastasis invades his whole body. My dad is no longer a strong man, he no longer screams with joy in front of the television when Olympique Lyonnais scores a goal, no longer laughs at Laurent Gerra's jokes, no longer meets his friends at the bistro on Sunday mornings, and no longer travels the roads of France at the wheel of his truck. He vegetates in the middle of the living room, sitting on a rocking chair, staring at the television set and zapping between animal documentaries and news. Mom is off work to take care of him. She has spent the last fifteen years of her life caring for patients in clinics and now she is at her husband's bedside.

- Hello, how are you doing my little mommy?

- It's okay, the nurse has just left the house, your father is resting in the room.

- She's coming Saturday morning to change the stoma, right? I'll be there too.

- Are you sure, my daughter? You already came last night, you're not going to travel another 200 km, I know that the road expenses are expensive.

- Don't worry my little mom, it's important for me to be there.

Even though my dad's illness and the fact that my parents live far away from my home never had any influence on my desire to prostitute myself, this money now allows me to stop counting my trips.

In a few weeks, I have become a woman in a hurry who juggles her agenda and her two identities. I have my conventional life, that of Mathilde who works from 9 am to 5 pm in an editorial office and whom her colleagues appreciate for her humor, but especially for her professionalism. Mathilde is known to her family and friends as a single woman who returns to her flat after work and spends all her weekends in the countryside with her family. Then there is Mathilda's life, who never leaves her work phone and who schedules appointments to entertain herself.

- Mathilde, do you remember the boys I met at the Sofitel, the night you were at your parents'? The band of friends who wanted two chicks. They invited us to London, it was the end of the Olympic Games and asked us to come. They don't pay us, but on the spot everything will be offered to us. Do you like it ? They were very nice.

- This is a great plan Coralie, I have never been to London and I need to disconnect, my father's condition is not getting any better.

I ask my dad for permission to go away for a weekend: "You think, girl, you're going to get rid of me in the space of 48 hours?"

On Friday, August 10, 2012, with Coralie, we meet Elijah, our host, at the easyJet terminal at Lyon-Saint Exupéry airport. I discover a very handsome young man, in his thirties, with the air of David Beckham in a more youthful way. His hair is dark blond, long on the top of his head and short on the sides. His eyes are brown and his look is lively, intelligent, mischievous, almost mischievous. A small, well-trimmed red beard outlines the fine contours of his face and gives him the touch of maturity that his young age lacks. His build is athletic and his tattooed arms give him a *bad boy* look. He has a catwalk and haute couture *street chic* style of dress, at the forefront of the latest trends. Givenchy T-shirt, Balmain jeans, Balenciaga sneakers, Breitling watch and Vuitton backpack. He would come out of a *shooting* for the cover of the next QG magazine that I would not be surprised. And in addition to being very handsome, he gives off something extremely nice, he is pleasant, smiling, pleasant and gentleman. He offers to carry our luggage, makes us pass in front of him, takes care of putting our stuff on the conveyor belt at the baggage check-in, offers us a cold drink at the *duty-free* and invites us to choose the seat we prefer in the plane. At first glance, this young man looks like the ideal son-in-law.

We got to know each other naturally during the hour of the flight. I have never met him in a professional context and I wanted to pay my airfare. I normally evolve in a framework of weekend between friends. He is single, childless, and the head of a small business in the transportation industry. He is from Lyon by adoption and at heart, but originally from Paris. We join his

9. Living for the better

closest childhood friends who have left to live and work in the City, on the other side of the Channel. I'm positive by nature, I like to meet people and easily pass on my energy, so with Elijah we quickly become friendly, almost familiar. His personality is attractive, atypical, he is the yin and the yang, the cop and the thug, the husband and the lover. Amateur of combat sports, he carries the values and advocates the surpassing of oneself. A believer, he regularly goes on spiritual retreats in the forest. A party animal, in love with women, the night and its excesses, he easily succumbs to nocturnal hijinks. He is everything and its opposite, but never strays from his convictions, never betrays what he is and those around him.

We arrive all three in London in a festive atmosphere. The weather was fine, the streets were full of tourists, and the city was decked out in the colors of the sporting event that was taking place. Our hosts, who were just like Elijah, picked us up at the airport in a brand new black Range Rover SUV and drove us to their home in the upscale Mayfair neighborhood. The boys live the high life, the apartment has three suites, the dressing rooms are overflowing with luxury clothes, bags and shoes. They collect Swiss watches and *street art*. Also in their thirties, in finance, they are welcoming, charming and benevolent. We are not obliged to do anything, neither to go out nor to sleep. They put at our disposal Ruinart, coke, weed and all that we desire at will. We toast to open the festivities of this weekend that promises to be warm and we tame each other to the rhythm of the glasses of champagne that we empty.

They are the new faces of the *escort* clientele. They are young, beautiful and rich. They wear three-piece suits during the day, smoke cigars at the end of business lunches, play golf on Sunday afternoons and order hookers and coke on Saturday nights. They live a wild and unbridled youth who deprive themselves of nothing and allow themselves everything. Paying a girl is the assurance of not having to worry about feelings. It is to be guaranteed to fuck without having to speak about love, future and tomorrow. Paying a girl is exciting. Calling on a stranger and exposing her, in the space of a moment, is said to be a powerful thing. They do not prohibit themselves anything, plan to three, to four. When they pay, it's to get a return on their investment! They live in abundance and consume the ass without limits. With us, they are charming, but not insistent, they are seductive and seductive.

We spend our time eating in the best restaurants of the city, drinking great wines, attending the most exclusive parties where only members of private clubs or athletes are invited. I drink with the legend Pele and dance with Michael Phelps. The boys have a small notoriety in the London night world. The bouncers greet us, the owners of the establishments make sure that we are well received. Our table is waiting for us in the VIP squares and, as the night goes on, the most extroverted English women flock there. We return from each evening as the sun rises. We were five when we left, we end up with fifteen in the apartment. I party, drink, smoke, but don't touch cocaine, I never use it, I am too afraid to like it. I dance and participate in the show with the other girls, between *champagne showers* and *booty shakes*, the temperature rises. I do what I like, what I feel like doing. I let myself be charmed sometimes by one and sometimes by the other, because a vacation without sex is like a mojito without

9. Living for the better

mint leaves. And it is the occasion to pull the pin, with this little sentence that we all said one day while leaving on vacation: "Everything that happens to, stays to".

- Mathilde, can you be more discreet? I remind you that these are my clients.

- Your customers? Me, they are my new friends, it's not about money. What bothers you? That I party?

- You always have to put yourself first, you can't help it. Well, go ahead and be a whore.

- Coralie, don't be mean or vulgar. I can remind you that a few weeks ago, you were the one they paid, you're the prostitute here tonight, it's not me.

We continue the stay without speaking to each other. The boys feel the discomfort, but give Coralie all the substances she wants to make her smile again. When we land in Lyon, she sends me a message while I'm still in the cab that takes me home.

- Don't ever call me again and keep on being a whore, it's sure made for you.

It's true that she and I don't approach this activity in the same way. I realize that she is undergoing it. Her speech of the first evening, where she praised it to me as being easy and attractive, evaporated as she dropped the mask. I discovered a new Coralie, bitter, jealous, sometimes hateful, and above all, ill at heart. Her mood is changeable, she can be adorable or hateful in an instant.

I am perfectly detached and I like my new status of desirable woman. It's a bit of revenge on the past. The fat cow has become an *escort*, like the caterpillar becomes a butterfly. Yesterday you didn't want me on your team, today you pay to have me in your bed.

I am the version of herself that disgusts her. She can't play the clean-cut middle-class girl with me anymore. I know who she is, what she does, she initiated me. When she sees me, she sees herself, this reflection that she hates so much, this environment that she tries to leave. She has been practicing for years and dreams of being a lawyer and a mother.

As a beginner, nothing affects me and I am able to assume my role perfectly, without shame or perversity.

Our collaboration and our friendship end here, on the tarmac of Saint-Exupéry airport. I go back to my appointments alone, with a slight bitter taste of a broken friendship.

Upon my return from London, I negotiate extra time off with the newspaper's director to be with my family full time. My dad is hospitalized again and on that Saturday afternoon, August 25, 2012, Johnny's greatest classics echo through the halls of the polyclinic.

- Dad, what do you want to hear?

He can no longer speak. He tries, but no sound will come out of his throat. He is fighting against himself. I see his tears running down his face. His body is unresponsive, but his brain and mind are fully present. He shakes his head and tries to communicate. He is annoyed, picks up the notebook on his bedside table and in capital letters, he writes:

"I'M GOING TO DIE"

The three of us, Mom, my sister and I, are in this clinic where Mom has spent her entire career, with the man of our lives who seems to be afraid of what he is the only one, at this moment, to realize.

He was not 56 years old. He died the next night. At dawn on a Sunday morning. At the time when he was getting up to open the trout fishing. At the time when we so often went to bed after wild parties. There will be no more *after parties*. He closed the evening, hand in hand with the one he loved so much. The glance fixing the sky, the smile to the lips, he left, it is mom who brought it to me.

"Live for the best, Want to give yourself everything, Richer for keeping nothing, Than love, Than love, Live to live free, Love all that you can love, Still and always want, Only love, Only love"[3] .

No child is prepared for the death of a parent, even if the illness is long and painful.

My mom stays the course, like the cats that hide to die, she waits for the evening to cry. We often say that when one person comes, another goes. And my sister's first daughter, 4 months old, is there to remind us that life must go on.

---

3. Johnny Hallyday, *Living for the best*.

10. A LIE THAT LASTS

September 2012

- I'm going to quit my job at the newspaper and move, Aurore.

- But, you just got a promotion and you love your job, why would you want to quit? It's hard to lose your daddy, but you're not going to leave everything overnight.

- This is not my life's work, I will find another. For now, I'm going to spend time with my mom, travel and get an apartment on my own, I've been living with you for over two years, it's time to move on.

- And how will you pay for it?

- I'll manage, I have savings.

- Mathilde, stop it, it's time you talked to me. I'm not stupid. I see how you've been living for several months. When we go to the restaurant, I see the cash you have. Do you think I'm going to judge you, that I don't care about you? And why did you and Coralie suddenly have a fight? I never really liked her, her condescending air tended to freeze me, but she was your friend.

I turn on my computer and show her my ad. I play it straight, as she asks me to do. For the first time, after six months of activity,

I confide, I almost confess. For the first time, I talk about prostitution to someone who is not linked to this environment or who has not met me in this context. She is interested, listens to my stories, questions me. The course of my appointments, the expectations of the men, the way they treat me, their profiles. Who are these men who pay and what are they looking for? How much are they willing to pay? How do they contact me? Are they all old and ugly? Do they have perverse practices? Do I feel dirty and cry sometimes? Do I come? Am I afraid, am I armed? Has anything happened to me? Do I protect myself properly and test regularly?

- So all your dates with Coralie, they weren't real?

- I'm sorry I lied to you, I didn't mean to upset you.

- Did she get you into this?

- No, not really.

For the first time, on her side, she has a direct experience with prostitution. She is fascinated, subjugated, her questions are flying and she drinks each of my words. She discovers this universe in a concrete way. It is no longer an illusory vision reported through a trashy reportage which lets imagine anything and everything, which only relates the extreme version of an environment prone to taboos, judgments, clichés and fantasies. She knows me, likes me, knows that I am not a lost girl or a *junkie*. I don't hate men, I haven't been raped or beaten. I have flaws, like any other human being, but I am an ordinary girl with an interesting job, who has decided of her own free will to move on to paid dating.

- I am amazed to discover that there is so much demand for this type of dating, and that girls like you do this, Coralie, Delphine, you. I thought it was a niche, in Monaco or Geneva. I know there are lots of trucks in Gerland, but it's not the same thing.

- Let's just say that the setting is different. Before, I had no idea how big this market was either. Since I have been immersed, I have a real and concrete estimate. I receive several hundred requests per month, so the percentage of men using this service is huge, it's not a fabrication. And the number of girls doing it occasionally or regularly is certainly in line with the demand. And as you say, girls like us, not only women under the influence of a pimp who are forced to work in a gloomy and violent world.

- But you still don't see a hundred clients a month?

- No, I don't see a hundred clients! I don't need many appointments to make a decent living.

- So you have cash stashed under your mattress like in the movies? Rhooo, come on, will you show me? Please!

I take out my little iron box, insert the key in the lock that locks it and hand it to her.

We are facing each other, sitting on the bed in my room. There is not a sound in the apartment. She looks me straight in the eye, holding it in her lap, she looks like a little girl on Christmas morning. She taps the metal with her fingertips and caresses it like Aladdin's lamp. After a few "Abracadabra", she opens it.

- Oh fuck! Ohhh fuck! But you're richer than the dealers down the block. Rhooo shit, I've never seen this much cash. Can I touch it? But how much do you have in there? But you bet it's worth it. Rhooo, it's great! I'm sorry, I'm a little excited right now, but hey, all that money!

I think most of us are like Scrooge at the sight of cash. We want to roll around in it, throw the bills in the air and shout "Place your bets, nothing's going to go wrong", light a cigar and pop a bottle of champagne, just because money gives you that fireworks-in-the-eye effect. Even when you don't care about money, you never remain insensitive to a bunch of banknotes spread out before you. Aurore wants to become a doctor to save lives, not to work in a private clinic and confuse prescriptions with bills. She is not accustomed to material things, doesn't care about having the latest iPhone, finds it ridiculous to spend even 15,000 euros on a car, when there are 5,000 that run very well. She likes to go on vacation with a backpack, a can of tuna and a bag of freeze-dried pasta. At this point, her excitement is more like finding a treasure, not the wealth that comes with it.

- And you have regulars?

- I'm starting to get a few.

- Can you tell me? I'm really curious to know, but if you don't like it...

- No, not at all, on the contrary I am happy to share this with you. There is Olivier. Actually, his name is Pierre-Jean. I discovered him not long ago, I saw his picture in *Le Progrès*.

- In the newspaper? What did he do?

- For his job, he is the director of a digital marketing school in Vaise. I already knew that, since we always meet in the premises.

- On the school premises? During school hours?

- No, in the evening. He tells me to meet him at 8:30. It's very strange, because the scenario is always the same, it's like going on vacation every year to the same place. I don't see what's so exciting and entertaining about it. Paying a girl to know exactly what's going to happen is not very exciting.

- And what happens during your meetings?

- He asks me to come without underwear.

- Certainly it excites him to know that you cross Lyon without panties.

- Maybe, but he knows I'm driving in. If I were to take the subway or if we were to go to a restaurant for dinner, I can imagine that it might be enticing in public, the side someone might notice if I put my hand up her skirt, I might have direct access to her little pussy. Now I don't know. And if it's the drive that turns him on, he'd be disappointed to know that I'm taking off my panties once I'm parked in the parking lot. Because in case of a car accident, arriving with the firemen at the hospital without underwear, I find that not very suitable!

- We see much worse in the hospital, you know! And besides the panties?

- When I arrive, we kiss each other goodbye and head to the drink machine. He puts in his little coins, presses the button for "sugar-free decaf" for me and "sweet coffee" for him. Then we go to a classroom and I sit on one of the desks, he stands facing me.

- He must be fantasizing about a naughty student turning him on without panties!

- I reassure you, his students enter the school with a bachelor's degree! I don't satisfy the fantasies of a pedophile pervert.

- Rhooo this is bad, I feel like I'm watching a show. Keep going!

- A porn series then, it turns you on little pig!

- I am unmasked, I hide, I am too ashamed.

- Get ready, what follows is great art! We drink our coffee, we usually discuss current events, his problems at work...

- Wait, let me cut you off, what does he look like? The principal of the school? The little fat guy with glasses and a bitter, jaded, vicious look?

10. A lie that lasts

- Definitely!

- I knew it!

- But no, definitely not! It's really a cliché. Olivier is tall, 1m80 with a nice look and a small belly. He's typically Mediterranean, I always feel like he's just come back from a fortnight in the tropics. His hair is brown, with a slight wave to the nape of his neck. He's in his early fifties, well preserved, he has a bit of BHL's physique when he was young, you know the type?

- BHL, he is not bad.

- Yes, but this is BHL from Lidl. It's the *low cost* version, I'm not going to exaggerate either.

- Is he married?

- I have no idea. He wears a wedding ring around his neck on a gold chain, but he has never told me anything personal about his life. I know he is from Brittany, he has a house in Brest where his parents live, but I know nothing else. Our discussions are mostly based on facts. When we finish our coffee, he comes up to me to kiss me and caresses my chest through my dress.

- Easy access, no bra required!

- Exactly, then he groped my crotch.

- Easy access, no panties!

- Exactly! I take his sex out of his pants. He still smells like soap, he has to wash himself before I get there, it's very appreciative.

- Doesn't he have any underwear?

- But yes, he has underpants and a belt! Excuse me, I'll cut this short. I'm not going to give you an exhaustive list of our outfits.

- Ah, but yes, I want all the details! Wait, you're doing BHL after all, Bernard Henri Lidl is not just anyone!

- It's clear! So BHL, who smells like soap, also has a big cock, since you want all the details, not really very long, but rather very thick. The kind of cock that makes your jaw hurt after five minutes of fellatio.

- I can see that. The ones that surprise you when you pull them out, where you back away and think, "Oh no, no, that's really not going to fit!"

- Yes, that's a bit of it.

- Do you use gel before taking off your panties? I'm talking technique, it's my doctor side. You're not mad at me?

- No, I don't use gel.

- Oh yeah, it fits by itself?

- No more.

- What do you mean, no more?

- Olivier does not penetrate me, ever. I lie on the desk, my buttocks on the edge of the table and my thighs open, like a gynecological examination. It's not very comfortable. He raises or removes my dress, with his fingertips plays with my clitoris without ever licking it. He has a way of caressing me which is rather unpleasant, he does not stimulate my clit, he irritates it! He puts his big sex on me, jerks off above my femininity, then I suck him for a few minutes before he resumes his hand game alone and ejaculates on my pubis or my breasts, always taking care to spread some all over me with his index finger. Many men do this, I wonder what goes on in their mind to like to smear us with their semen. I'd have to find out more, but I guess it's probably still related to domination! With his pants around his ankles in a duck-like gait, he heads to the bathroom and brings me some paper to clean myself up, although most of the time

I get out a pack of wipes before he comes back. He gets dressed, finally, pulls up his shorts and pants, because he didn't take anything off, and walks me to the exit. Less than fifty minutes pass between my arrival on the parking lot and my departure.

- Is that all? He pays to jerk off? You sold me great art, but this is a Sunday night erotic movie on M6 in the 1990s. I'm disappointed.

- This leaves me as perplexed as you. Maybe it's the context that excites him or that a few caresses mixed with human warmth allow him to escape and meet his needs and desires. It's not a very glamorous appointment, no palace or champagne, just a handjob with a companion, but he is always very kind to me.

Olivier is an educated, courteous, friendly man. He says he is happy to see me, enjoys my company and our discussions. On my side, I have the feeling to bring him a little happiness, and having regulars is pleasant, to weave links and to go beyond the tariff side. When I don't hear from him for several weeks, I send him a short text message to see how he's doing, and then he schedules an interview. Being interested in and concerned about the other person makes these meetings real human encounters. I know it may sound crazy, but the more the months go by, the more the meetings follow each other, the more I have the feeling that these men buy my time, my company more than my body.

- I shouldn't say this, but I think you are right. I don't see what the problem is. We can dispose of our bodies as we wish. It takes a lot of balls to do that, no pun intended. But like you, there's not much to stop you. On the other hand, you can't have just that as a life, you don't make a career out of being an *escort*, and you know that you have abilities that allow you to have an exciting future. Promise me, Mathilde, that you won't sink.

- I'm taking a break for a few months. I'm not going to lie to you, Aurore, it's hard to get up every morning, to find the motivation to earn in a month what I earn now in a few hours. I don't feel like working at the newspaper anymore, I'm bored and overworked. I'm going to take a year off, use this freedom to travel with my mom and I'll see where it takes me, I have faith in myself.

- Count on me to call you to order. And I don't suppose your mother and sister know about it. You know, Mathilde, a lie that lasts too long is often difficult to accept.

My mother is a modern woman with whom one can discuss, she does not expect me to fit into a mold, she has given up the idea. She doesn't expect me to tell her every secret I have. She knows I am too independent to call her every morning and tell her everything that is going on in my life.

- And your daughter Mathilde, what is she doing? What is she doing? Does she finally have a sweetheart?

- Oh, Mathilde, she's doing her little life, she'll eventually find her way and settle down.

An iron hand in a velvet glove, this is an expression that fits perfectly to this French-Italian woman that is my mother, this independent woman and pioneer of feminism. She is a young adult in the seventies, she is part of the first generation to be able to take contraception, to have an abortion, to live her sexuality freely, to wear mini-skirts without it shocking anyone, and to sunbathe topless on the beaches without being considered depraved. To work, to earn her own money, not to depend on a man and not to be limited to cooking and giving birth: "Be free my girls". That's what she taught us, and even if I always tend to push the envelope a little too far, whatever she says, I follow her guidelines.

11. Mathilde, tell us a story

Now I'm alone on my boat. Since Coralie left, I no longer have a chaperone. We kept each other informed of our appointments, it was our safety net, we knew who, where, how long. Even though I never had to call her, it's reassuring to have someone who knows, especially for a beginner who hasn't yet mastered all the ins and outs of this business. And even if Aurore is now in the know, I can't give her the role of security guard.

From time to time, on Saturday evenings, I meet her with her college friends. They aspire to become surgeons, emergency physicians, general practitioners, and anesthetists, and they all have to combine their studies with their shifts at the hospital.

We laugh, dance, sing. One of them takes the guitar and the others start the last hymn they composed about the hospital's adventures. Usually, the stories are gloomy, even downright scandalous, but with a bit of humor and a few notes of music, the story becomes amusing. And that's how this poor granny who was raped by a homeless man in her room, in the geriatric ward, became our mascot during our evenings a little too drunk, on the tune of Cookie Dingler, the liberated woman turned into:

"Tonight in the emergency room, Granny is asleep, in a hospital bed, waiting to die, but you don't care, you rape her anyway and whisper to her "Shut up, old lady". And I raped granny and she liked it, and she's waiting for tomorrow to do it again.

Poor granny, and poor goat too. The patient of one of them, who came in for a consultation with acute headaches, thought it necessary to give her information that he thought might be related:

- Doctor, I must tell you that I make love to my goat. Maybe that's what's causing my headaches?

- Okay, I see. But no, sir, I don't think it's related and I'm not sure I'm competent for this pathology. I can possibly advise you to find a colleague who is more specialized in the relationship with animals.

- Oh yes, there are doctors who specialize in sex with animals?

- In the relationship with the animal, I meant in the behavior to adopt with the animals. Forget it, I'll write you a prescription for a consultation.

Compared to that, the man who asks me to urinate on him, it's cat pee!

They tell me about their adventures and, under the cover of my personal life and a deceptively active Adopteunmec account, I tell them about mine. It has become a little ritual. In the middle of the evening, they all chant together:

- Mathilde, tell us a story!

- You think I'm Papa Bear?

It's true that something always happens to me, more or less unpleasant anecdotes, in my everyday life or during my meetings. When it's not the baker who kindly takes an interest in me and asks me questions:

- Are you married? Do you have children?

- No, neither of them.

- Oh, but you're all alone? Still at your age? Divorced perhaps, at least? she said to me in a frightened tone. Here, I offer you a bag of croissants.

I don't know if I find it nice or miserable: "Here, poor girl, go drown your loneliness in a crusty butter plate".

When it's not her, it's a friend's buddy who, in an *after party at* his place, at 5 o'clock in the morning coming back from a party, tells me:

- Well, now I want to fuck you.

- I just came to have a nightcap, you know.

- You are in my house, if I want to fuck you, I'll fuck you. I don't ask for your opinion. You shouldn't have come.

The two young men fought, I ran away, I wandered down St. Catherine Street until I found a cab, my makeup dripping and my tights spun.

Then, this time I stayed at a pseudo-lover's house. At 3 a.m., I was awakened by loud knocks on the front door and by women's voices:

- Jefferson, open up, we know it's there.

Jefferson already had two wives, and now they were ganging up on me.

- Come out, we won't hurt you.

- I'd rather not, no. But, you know girls, I didn't know you existed. Don't worry, when I can get out of here safely, when it's quiet again, I'll leave it to you!

And in the middle of all this, I slip my girlfriends a pretty, almost romantic rhyme, which is only the result of a paid encounter.

- A few years ago, I met a boy when I was living near Bordeaux, a soccer player, extremely sexy.

- A pro? Do we know him? Who is he?

- Girls, who follows soccer? Which one can give me the name of a player?

- Zidane!

- Besides Zidane? A player from Bordeaux? No, no one? A Lyonnais perhaps?

- Yes, yes, I have, wait, what's his name? Everybody knows it. Yes, I do. A redneck, handsome guy, it'll come back to me.

- So we agree, no one knows anyone, it's not useful for me to reveal his identity.

- A photo, a photo, a photo!

- Maybe afterwards if you're good and I can tell my story without having a bunch of half-hysterical girls interrupting me every ten seconds.

- Wait, let's have another drink!

- This is going to be a juicy story, I'm sure.

- Can I start again? So, Mario calls me last week. It's a pseudonym, so don't start Googling. He's visiting Lyon and would like to meet up. Mario is tall, Mario is handsome, Mario is muscular and quick-witted, when the ball arrives at his feet, he knows he has to run!

- First tackle! You're off to a great start, poor guy.

- I met him at the Villa Florentine, in the heights of Lyon, for a drink.

- Did you put yourself in a bomb?

- On top! I am at the top of my game, I am the sixth star of the hotel!

- But how you show off! But how I love it when you tell the stories! We feel like we are there.

- The concierge greets me: "Hello ma'am, hello sir". And then I see this divine creature, this modern-day apollo, the well-named Mario, arrive, his hat pulled down to the middle of his eyes and his sunglasses on. The crowd moves away. Finally, the cleaning lady who passes by shifts. He walks straight towards me. I feel like chanting his name as if I were entering a match. He gives me a little hug before addressing the concierge: "Can you call the driver to take us down to the Presqu'île? Right away, Mr. Mario." The hotel's tinted-window Jaguar arrives a few moments later. We slip inside. And what do you think, girls, is the first thing I say to him?

- Where are we going?

- It's good to see you, since the time?

- Fuck me right now on the bench?

- That's what I thought! That's not what I told him!

- Knowing you, you must have given him the guided tour of Lyon. On your right, you can see the magnificent basilica of Fourvière, just next to it, the mini Eiffel tower which, in fact, more vulgarly, is none other than a satellite antenna. Do you know why we celebrate December 8th?

- Do you have any friends for my girlfriends?

- Come on, you're making us wait, what did you say to him?

- I said, "But are you serious? Did you have to put an umbrella over your head and put on sunglasses when it was dark? Do you really think that someone will recognize you? We are in Lyon and you are not Benzema!

- Ah here it is, Benzema! That's the name I was looking for earlier! So it's not him ?

11. Mathilde, tell us a story

- But is it really known?

- Like a soccer player. He looked at me and said, "I'll take it all off when we sit down to eat. Perverse thoughts running through my mind, of course! Everything humm, I don't ask so much from you! The driver stopped in double file in front of the restaurant before opening the door for me. Mario, head down, got out in turn. We had to walk five meters to reach the restaurant. Two passers-by arrived at the same time and said to him: "Hey, Mario, just because you're hiding under a cap doesn't mean we don't recognize you. Shall we take a selfie? Miss, are you coming in the picture? Uh no, that's okay, thanks!" When the two fans left, I said, "Well, see, that's exactly what I was telling you five minutes ago. There's no point in dressing up, no matter what happens you'll be recognized. When you're a star, you're a star!"

- But you are of a legendary bad faith, remarkable even!

- I must admit that it made me laugh.

- And what does a footballer eat?

- Grass, to be at one with the land! No, he took me to Cuisine et Dépendances, rue de la Charité, next to Bellecour, the gastronomic table of Chef Fabrice Bonnot. It was the first time I was faced with a menu without prices. Quite honestly, it's not easy to make a choice.

- What is the problem? It's armored.

- Yes, but even though it may seem elegant, in reality it is very awkward. First of all, because you are the woman and therefore the restaurant owner assumes that you will be invited.

- Did you intend to pay?

- Absolutely not! But that doesn't mean that the price doesn't interest me. So I ordered the same thing he did, the "Prestige

Mille et Une Saveurs" menu. Mise en bouche, two starters, two main courses, cheese, dessert and mignardises. Believe me, after all that, you have to be pretty athletic to still have energy for a body to body!

- So he scored a goal?

- If he had been a rugby player, I would have told you that he scored a try, but did not convert it!

This charming sportsman was very pleasant, I left in the middle of the night with my envelope, but that, except for Aurore, my girlfriends do not know it. One story leads to another, we never talked about Mario again. He was directly put in the "one night stand" box, keeping his anonymity. But, the truth is that I don't have a one-night stand anymore. Do we want to fuck when we are prostitutes? For my part, yes, but not in any way, not with just anyone, not for mediocre and sloppy sex. If I decided to choose this way of meeting people, it's precisely to avoid all these bland one night stories. So, from now on, the rare times I accept to offer myself to a man, it's purely selfishly, for my only pleasure, without caring about my partner or the next day or what he thinks of me. I live the role reversal and it is a position that seems obvious to me, almost a fair return of behaviors, a boomerang thrown years ago by these gentlemen and that had to come back sooner or later having made a 180 degree turn.

- Mathilde, you're really a great girl, I love spending time with you. Do you want to go away together next weekend? And tomorrow at noon, will you come to lunch with me at some friends' place?

- Yes, with great pleasure. I too enjoy the moments we share.

- Are you staying over?

- No, that's nice, I'll go home. I'll meet you tomorrow for lunch at your friends' house.

- Finally, I prefer to go alone.

This anecdote lived with a personal courtier is revealing of today's society and our relationships between men and women. We consume people as we consume things. If you don't have sex, you're not interesting, if you have sex, you're not interesting anymore. Because a few months before, this same young man had given me the big game. I had succumbed and stayed "asleep", then he had vanished. I'm not saying that love doesn't exist, I just think that having too many easy choices doesn't make us choose anymore. We don't make an effort anymore, we don't fight, we *swipe* and we *ghost*. *Ghosting* has become the new trend. People disappear without a word, without explanation or reason, whether in love or friendship. I've often felt like that iPhone, which is only a few months old and whose screen isn't even cracked, but which is put away because the latest one has a new option, which has no use, but which makes it more attractive. To justify his behavior after I refused to sleep with him, this suitor accused me of:

- You offended me. Your rejection of me made me think that you were indifferent to me, so I didn't want you to come to lunch so as not to force you to spend time with me.

- Isn't that a spoiled child's reaction? For my part, it seems to me that when you try to seduce someone with real, honest, sincere feelings, you don't stop at a declining sex game. Besides, remember when we spent a night together, you didn't call me back. What explanation do you have for that? Was I too interested in you?

- I didn't want to abuse you, I just wanted to be romantic and spend the night in your arms.

- Forgive me, it is true that I don't have much notion in terms of romance. It seemed to me that this one was linked to seduction, patience, flowers and small kind messages.

12. WHERE I WANT, WHEN I WANT

October 2012, my resignation from the newspaper is effective.

- Math', will we see each other again? Don't worry about Coralie, she's got some problems...

- She did what she thought was right. You know, my Delphine, friends come and go, and only time can guarantee a sincere friendship.

- She couldn't stand that life anymore.

- I was not a client, but her friend.

Between the doors of our respective offices, our half-word conversation is enough. I wink at him, my box of personal belongings under my arm, all my memories of these three years at this newspaper that I loved so much. Journalists, layout artist, accountant, salesmen, the excitement of the closing days, the Friday pizzas, my name in the bear, I will miss this atypical universe, but from now on I am completely free. I cross the Place des Cordeliers, I might as well be in New York. I take height and see myself treading the cobblestones with my heels, my head lightly rocked by the wind breeze and my cheeks warmed by the last rays of the autumn sun. Tonight, I don't take a cab, I squeeze into the C3 bus that takes me home: "Hi, artists! A new life is offered to me".

The following weeks, I navigate between Lyon, my research of apartment, my appointments and stays at my mom's. One evening, we are comfortably on her sofa, a glass of burgundy in the hand in front of a report of the program *Seven to Eight* in which testifies with hidden face an *escort* of Geneva. My mother comments:

- If I were 30 years old today, I would choose this lifestyle.

- Oh, yes? My little mother, I knew your broad-mindedness, but not your loose morals!

- Slight morals, but finally my daughter, sexual freedom is a right.

- But, when you get paid, freedom becomes a job, right?

- So what? If it is a choice, it makes even more sense, the freedom to work is also a right.

I know my mom well enough to know that her remarks are not insignificant.

- I'm visiting an apartment tomorrow.

- Considering getting a new job to pay the rent?

- Not at the moment, I've been unemployed for less than a month.

- Mathilde, my daughter, how much longer do you think your lovers will be generous with you?

- The time to find one who will love me.

My answer sounds like a confession, and we don't need to expand on it. What seemed like a possibility to him becomes a reality at that moment. But, I hide behind a laughing tone to sow some doubts.

My roommate Aurore and I have no problems, and I want my apartment to receive my clients. Appointments on the road take more time and I am regularly confronted with "fantasists". Even if I talk for several minutes on the phone with each man and try to detect the personality behind the screen, my technique is unfortunately not infallible.

The "fantasist" discusses at length, goes into the details of the sexual performance. He is insistent, evokes all the positions, the ejaculation, questions me on my various lingeries, exposes me his wish of *dress code*. When we agree on the modalities of the appointment, which takes place in the stride, he continues the exchanges by messages. Either kindnesses: "You have a very beautiful voice, I am happy to meet you. Or details about my preferences and my pleasure: "I want to make you come, how do you want me to take you?" He never breaks the contact until the time of the meeting. When I send the message: "I am parked", he does not answer anymore. And if I try to call, he turns off his phone. Men fantasize, and since it's easier to talk about sex with a prostitute than with a Tinder girl, they pretend to meet, masturbate during the exchange and then disappear. It's infuriating, but that's the job that comes in: learning to analyze behavior and knowing how to say no to a date request when it seems suspicious, even if it isn't, knowing how to say no. In my business, this is the most important thing. I am also learning, with experience, that the hour-to-hour meetings are there to satisfy a sexual impulse, the animal impulse of a man who wants to unload. He doesn't want to buy you a glass of wine or know if you have a side business or if you've had ten clients in one day. He doesn't care, he wants to fuck. You're not a delicious pastry he's treating himself to, you're just a common Sodebo sandwich.

I set out to find the ideal accommodation to receive guests at home, but in complete security and discretion. After several months of searching, in May 2013, I signed the lease of a T2 cours Émile Zola in Villeurbanne. The building had just been completed and I was the first tenant. When I visited it, workers were still working on it and not all the floors were finished. There is a videophone, a double security lock, a code to access the elevator, a second code to operate it and go up to the floors. But what appeals to me the most is the location.

- Hello, Elijah? You can't imagine where I'm going to put my boxes!

- You've found an apartment, congratulations my dear! So, where is it?

- At the police station! Finally, the building next to the police station!

- But this is huge! You might even start dealing! Because you know what they say: you can't see what's in front of you!

- That's exactly it! For the deal, it seems way too dangerous to me, to each his own, but I couldn't have found a better home.

Since London, with Elijah, we have become friends. It's not about sex or money, he is my pillar, the big brother I never had, one of the men in my life. The one I would choose if there was only one left. Frank, honest, straightforward, lucid, open-minded and a fighter. We did not develop any romantic feelings, but a great friendship. I know everything about him, he knows everything about me.

I moved in June 2013, certain that I was not unsafe by stating, "This is the building stuck to the police station. My balcony looks directly out onto the backyard where police officers smoke their cigarettes, eat lunch in the sun or exercise. If there is a problem, I simply open the window. And you'd have to be pretty damn peachy to come in and murder or rob anyone living in the most secure, camera-ridden area of the city. It's a bit cheeky, but I find the prospect of having men next to a concentration of law enforcement amusing.

I am no longer a beginner or a casual. I did my first trick over a year ago, and my only business for the past nine months has been prostitution. I bring men to my house and nothing ever happens to me. I am becoming more and more selective and I don't receive many. I offer this service as a last resort and am almost certain that the person is trustworthy. It is both convenient and confusing to be in the home. Convenient from an organizational point of view, I don't have the commute time and make less effort to dress myself. If I wear a dress that is a little too short, tight and my stockings are showing, I don't run into anyone anyway. In case of a bunny, I don't move from my house, but there is no magic of five star hotels, champagne bubbles and chocolates that come with them. For the men who come to my place, it's *all inclusive*, like in a Maramara club. I have to offer them a drink, and very few of them arrive with a bottle in hand. One day, one of them offers me a bottle of perfume, *J'adore* by Dior, a nice wink, but I have been wearing *Coco Mademoiselle* since I was 18. And I'm not going anywhere, I'm waiting for a man. The purpose is the same, but, as with everything, there is the art and the way. I don't mind having sex in my bed, I always put on a rag and wash it after each encounter. What does bother me is the lack of charm and prestige of home meetings. So

12. Where I want, when I want

I continue my escapades in hotels and in men's homes. I make friends with some and am almost a girlfriend to others, although I distance myself from men who have too much affection for me. I do not wish to play with feelings for financial gain. Honesty and caring must go both ways for a healthy relationship.

When I get tired of Lyon, I go to Nice, I change the location of my ad and rent on Booking an apartment with a sea view, on the Promenade des Anglais. This is one of the attractive aspects of this activity, and I always come back to this word: freedom. To be able to go anywhere, anytime, to follow your desires, the sunshine or the snowy slopes. To decide to bask in the sun or to meet people to finance your vacation.

Between two appointments, I walk on the sand and have lunch on the terrace of the Negresco. I like to escape to Nice, the city is beautiful, the weather is always nice. I'm thinking of moving there, and out of curiosity I browse the Pôle emploi website. I discovered an offer for a sales position in the advertising sector. I'm at Place Masséna in a café at breakfast time:

- Mrs. Davril, you have just applied for our offer, would you be available to exchange a few minutes?

- Yes, with pleasure.

- It is a job of itinerant salesman on the Paca region. We guarantee you an advance of the minimum wage, which will then be deducted from your commissions, and you will have a company car at the end of your six-month trial period, if your sales figures are high enough to cover this expense.

- So, I use my vehicle to tour the whole region and if I don't make enough money, I go into debt to your company, right? It makes me think of pimping, doesn't it?

Perhaps I am too ambitious or dreamy to accept anything, but the reality of the job market leaves me confused and confirms me in the idea that my choice of life is much more rewarding, libertarian and remunerative. I would rather sell my body and my time and be the sole beneficiary than feel like I am prostituting myself for a boss.

In July 2013, I agreed to meet Nicolas, 36 years old. He invites me to meet him in his hotel room, an Ibis outside of downtown Nice. It's not a palace, but the young man *books* me for two hours and took care to ask me what my preferences were, wine, champagne, soda, chips or cashews, details that make a difference and foreshadow a festive moment.

When he opens the door for me, I take a step back. I am facing "the neighborhood guy". He has the whole stereotype: the Lacoste jogging suit, the backwards cap, the pair of Air Max and the joint in his hand. Nevertheless, he tries to reassure me.

- First of all, I want to apologize. My name is Bilel, not Nicolas. But since girls like you don't want to meet guys like me, I lied about my name. I know there are a lot of losers out there and I totally understand. But I'm a cool guy. I just want to have a good time, without the hassle. Tonight you are my princess. If you want some shit, there is some, some coke too. I got champagne, I got Jack, and if you need anything, I'll make a call and you'll get everything you want. I'm paying you right now, if you want to hide the money in your stuff or put it in your car, there's no problem, go ahead, I'll wait. If you come back, it's fine, if you don't come back, you'll be the bad guy.

He's right, girls like me usually don't want to meet guys like him. As far as I'm concerned, I've never discriminated on the basis of first name, if the man introduces himself in a friendly way, uses a sustained vocabulary and invites me to a residential area, then I give him my trust, just like anyone else.

I spend a completely lunar evening with this exuberant and extravagant personality. I don't take any of the drugs that are spread out on the bedside table, I have to remain in full possession of my means. Being clear-headed and responsive at all times is one of my self-imposed rules. I smoke cigarettes and sip champagne. He rolls joints, hits traces of cocaine, pours glass after glass of whiskey and tells me his stories. He would be the head of the business in Nice, everything goes through him. He tells me about the organization of the network in France, in Morocco, the role of each one, the wars of territories, the techniques to make pass the drug, the prison.

- We just tried a shot, but it didn't go well. That's why I need to disconnect tonight, baby. This is going to cost me dearly for this crap. Three months ago, I was introduced to a helicopter pilot who wanted to go rogue. Since I'm always looking for new ways to smuggle cannabis, I set up a deal. The helicopter was to pick up 200 kilos in the mountains of the Hassi Berkane area, south of Melilla, and fly them up to Sainte-Léocadie, a village on the other side of Andorra. We worked like crazy on this mission, with my teams. Landing a helicopter in the Moroccan mountains, you can imagine that it doesn't go unnoticed and that in less than five minutes all the local military land. We had to come to an agreement with them, pay them to close their eyes. We bought lights, beacons, everything necessary to make the helicopter land and take off in the dark, and motorcycles to watch with infrared binoculars.

- Quite an organization. But with all these investments and the helicopter, is it profitable?

- Yes, you make money on several transactions.

- What went wrong, did the chopper crash?

- No, I trusted a badger. I'll tell you something, sweetie, when you don't master a field, you don't jump into it, I've learned that. But it was such a beautiful shot, I let my ego get the better of me. Passing drugs by helicopter, it made me dream! I would have taken it to the next level in the business.

- Did the pilot hijack the cargo?

- He wouldn't have had the balls to do it, excuse me, sweetheart, I'm talking dirty.

- What did he do? You're making me long for this!

- He left France with the chopper, officially for a tourist flight. He flew over Spain and then crossed the Alboran Sea to land in Melilla, on the African continent, but it is a Spanish city. He had to refuel and cross the border. Only, this moron was not aware that prior authorization was required to cross from Spain to Morocco, and getting that authorization takes several weeks. He had to turn back empty.

- This is amateurism! Excuse me, but setting up an operation like this and getting stopped for a paperwork issue is like doing a robbery with an electric scooter without a battery!

- That's not the worst of it. Since the chopper didn't come, the merchandise was seized. Everything had to be clean at 6 am. The military broke our agreement and took the drugs away. I still have to pay my supplier, it's my transportation that got screwed up.

- It must be a huge debt, 200 kilos, 200,000 euros?

12. Where I want, when I want

- In this range! I'm negotiating, but you don't mess with people like that. This morning, there were three guys from Marseille downstairs, sent by the Moroccans, Kalash in hand. They came to tell me the amount of the bill, the deadline to pay and they are looking for the driver. They want to smoke him.

- You bet! He must not be serene.

- I told him to go hide until it blows over. I'm a nice guy, you know, sweetheart, I'm not going to get a family man killed.

- That's a nice story. Tell me again, there were armed thugs in front of your house this morning and they want to kill someone. When I leave, when I open the door, will I get shot?

- No, sweetheart, don't worry! Don't forget that I'm the boss and this is my town.

I'm still dressed, he didn't do any search. I can be a cop. I don't talk to him about it. I don't want to arouse suspicions that don't exist. He tells me everything or tells me a movie script, I don't know, but he goes so far as to take a .44 Magnum out of his stuff. I'm not afraid of firearms, I've already done some shooting in training ranges and I've been here for almost two hours, I don't feel insecure. The young man is eager to confess and I am passionate about his stories. It's my turn to be at the heart of exclusive investigations, of this world as hidden as mine. A little more exposed it's true, we do more hunting for narcotics than for whores, there are more reports on drug dealers than on *escort girls*.

He adds money to me so that I stay one more hour. He doesn't touch me, he doesn't kiss me, he's not interested in my body, he wants to get high and tell me about his life. He adds money to me again and again and certainly ends up thinking: "Maybe I should fuck her, that's why I brought her here in the first place." But, it's already too late, his body is full of substances that prevent the proper functioning of his male body.

Each time I come to Nice, I inform him of my presence. Every time he changes his phone number, he gives it to me. From time to time we spend a few hours together, similar to the first ones, with more and more incredible stories.

But in Nice, beyond the atypical encounters and the view on the sea, it is the solitude which gives rhythm to my stays. Seeing men and having lunch alone is not very pleasant for long. I need emotional and friendly links, a girlfriend to spend my money with in Monaco. So I scoured the *escorting* websites. I find Sandra's ad which seems to have the same profile as mine. I send her a message of presentation and in the stride she calls me to have a drink. We meet on the terrace of a small discreet bar in the old Nice. She is a very beautiful, slender young woman, her long, wavy, bright red hair, her large green eyes with perfectly curved lashes and her porcelain complexion make her look like Princess Ariel, the Little Mermaid, even though she confided to me that she did not appreciate this comparison, which seems to be flattering. She has a pure, Nordic and natural beauty. She is originally from Nice, is 30 years old and is in professional reconversion. Coming from a wealthy background, very elegant and refined, she has always been in the world of luxury and knows Monaco and its faults perfectly. Being an *escort* when you are single is almost normal on the French Riviera. It starts with a proposal from a generous businessman at the Buddha-bar, an exchange of courtesies disguised as gallantry. Then it becomes recurrent, because just as I think, why offer yourself when some men are ready to pay? This awareness then becomes an evidence and a way of life. Right away, she shows sympathy towards me, she is funny, benevolent, advises me on the districts to avoid, gives me the phone numbers of men with problems. On some *escorting* sites, there is a "Blacklist" section. The girls can list the numbers, leave a comment, a description of the men who have behaved badly. Theft, rape, violence, sequestration, dark stories are told. Before validating an appointment, I systematically check the number on the online *listing*. We are usually alone and isolated in our art, so when we meet fellow women or a way to be connected, solidarity takes over our so-called competition or female jealousy.

13. MASTER IN SEX

I spent the end of 2013 going from Lyon to Nice, Aix-en-Provence and Paris.

Sandra, my new *escort* girlfriend, makes me discover Monaco, the restaurants, the Caffé Milano, the Maya Bay, the casino, the night, the Jimmy'z, the Buddha-Bar. I observe a new face of prostitution, the ultra luxury. All the clubs are filled with young women who could easily claim to be the muse of Victoria's Secret. They are among friends, dancing, singing and speaking English. As the evening progresses, businessmen, Russian or Saudi for the most part, flock in and, when the valet brings forward Ferrari or other Lamborghini, the ladies follow the pace.

I have never worked in Monaco. I can't compete with them, I don't have the looks and I don't speak a word of English. But I go out for dinner and drinks with Sandra. We are certainly still registered, several times at the entrance to the city we were checked: identity papers, profession.

- What are you ladies doing in Monaco? You come to meet men?

- No, officer, we're coming to dinner.

Even if it was true, we still got the suspicious look and the little phrase as we left:

- Don't let them find you in a hotel.

I have never worked in a duo with Sandra, my experience with Coralie has cooled me down. However, as two friends, we share our free time, beach, shopping, restaurant, discussions about the world, men, politics, as any woman, which we are.

I have been a prostitute for over a year and a half and am now a sex expert. The demands and expectations of men no longer hold any secrets for me, whether I realize them or not. I now have a global vision of sexuality. I know what I'm good at, I've discovered my talents and I know how to fulfill everyone's desire while having fun. Nevertheless, as for women, I realize that each man has different desires and sensitivities, but that his feminine side is never far away:

"Lick my nipples. Nibble them, roll them between your fingers and pinch them gently. Hummmm yes, oh yes, hummm, still don't stop, keep going, oh yesiiiii".

It's not very manly to have a man moaning like a girl while having his nipples licked. I didn't know that it could bring so much pleasure to the opposite sex. I know how sensitive my breasts are, but I didn't know it could be increased tenfold in a man, to the point that I didn't want anything else.

"I hate getting blown".

Oh yes? There are men who don't like to be sucked? Great discovery. But it's a rare species, I've only met two specimens in this style. Maybe they had been bitten before! If my lover didn't like this introduction, I think I would be unhappy. It's kind of like having an ice cream cone in your hand and watching it melt. If I had known, I would have taken a small jar!

"Pull my balls up. Harder!"

Ouch! No? Just like those practices with clothespins on the nipples or on the clitoris. But, ouch! I don't know at what point pain becomes pleasure. Take spanking, for example, I like it. Getting it, not giving it! However, not all spankings are pleasant, there is a real technique, the position of the hand, the energy, the intensity, the frequency and the poetry that goes with it. But perhaps sexual characteristics are like gastronomic characteristics, because when you see a snail, an oyster or a sea urchin, it is not very tasty, but you just have to taste it...

"Can you stroke my hair when I lick you?"

Oh a blanket! What a silky hair you have! Can I suck my thumb at the same time and twist your hair between my fingers? Personally, I prefer to have my hair pulled, but it seems that it is not said.

"Can you go down, more, even lower?"

You want me to lick your crack and put a finger in it, is that right? All those who have tried, liked, tried again and many do not say a word, but at the moment of fellatio raise their buttocks to call out.

I have never done it, to anyone, neither in the pro nor in the perso, never tongue nor finger, no caress or massage lower than the birth of the buttocks. I don't say "fountain", but indeed, one can be an *escort* and quite chaste, not really frigid, a bit dirty, but not completely without taboo!

"Hello, Mathilde, let me introduce myself, I'm Alex, 44 years old, 180/80, brown hair, blue eyes, married, dynamic executive.

Heteroflexible, my desire is for role reversal, with dildo belt. Accustomed to the libertine environment and to the fact that madam wears the belt, I am looking for an accomplice to accompany us. If the presence of the lady is a brake, I am looking for two accomplices to replace her.

Heteroflexible? I think it's the same as flexitarian! And when you google it, the first definition is: to be flexitarian is to do without anything.

I find this attractive. But as for the role reversal, I'm at a loss. The image doesn't excite me, but it doesn't disgust me either. I prefer dominant males, that's for sure. I am too resistant to authority in life, being authoritarian and demanding myself. So in bed, I need to be channeled, to find the right balance.

"I like it when a woman gives me orders. You could force me to do your housework and punish me by stepping on me in stilettos if I don't obey properly."

Walking in high heels on asphalt is already not very natural or obvious, it requires a little training, so on a human body, without having taken the balancing act option at the baccalaureate, it seems far too dangerous!

- Do you accept facial and oral ejaculations?

- Before answering, I have a question. What attracts you to these practices?

- I think it's the porn movies.

- Are you an actor?

- No!

- Well, I'm not an actress either...

I also learned to deal with bodies, morphologies, differences and the injustice of Mother Nature.

"We spoke on the phone earlier. I wanted to clarify something for you. I am particularly fond of foreplay, taking care of my partner, cunni, fingering, clitoral massage, because I am not mounted like a god! It's rather the opposite, with a lot of precocity, I'm not a marathoner."

It's a bit of a losing jackpot! Precocity can be controlled. On the other hand, does the size count? Because there, there is nothing to do. I believe that yes, a little bit, because even if a micropenis manages to satisfy you by playing with the excitement and that certain positions support the clitoral pleasure, something is missing. I have had lovers in this situation, the problem is that I never liked to suck my thumb...!

I've dealt with medium yards more often than the extremes, but there's one common trend among them, the zero cut. A hairless body reduces the risk of odor and limits hair loss in the mouth.

What about the fat ones? The ones for whom Skin has invented the "King Size" condoms! They are strong, the guys in the communication department, I imagine them in a meeting in front of a *paperboard* making drawings and word associations to find the commercial name of the product. But, are those called "TBM", the Very Well Mounted, guaranteed 100% orgasm? Is this really a guarantee of satisfaction? An instant and tenfold enjoyment by a member of gargantuan dimensions? It would be too simple and beautiful if I said yes. But no, as said above, the size counts, but it's not too much!

- Mathilde, to be an *escort*, you have to love sex?

- But, to be relaxed in life, you have to like ass! And also to be happy in couple, especially if you don't like to cook!

13. Master in sex

I'm often like a sexologist in conversations with my girlfriends and boyfriends, but I have knowledge of the field, not books.

- Mathilde, how do you do it? With my artichoke heart, I'm sure I would fall in love on almost every date!

- I think, Aurore, that the money between us allows us not to exceed the limits. It's a kind of guarantee. They pay me to love them for an hour, but when the time is up, the coach turns into a pumpkin. And my phone rings Monday through Thursday basically, starting on Friday, they're with madam.

- Do you think all men are unfaithful?

- I know that 80% of my clients are couples.

- Yes, well, you ladies are also unfaithful! I have more than one mistress who is married!

- But you, Elijah, it's because you are a stud, no woman can resist you. And you're a fucker, you can feel it! And since most guys can't make us come, we see you as a hope!

- Ah, Mathilde! You know, my darling, that I love you and how fabulous it is to have an *escort* girlfriend! I should enjoy it more often!

- When we see each other, I'm off duty!

As there is always an exception to the rules, my speech about the distance between the *escorts* and the clients does not hold anymore when Sandra calls me.

- Mathilde, Fred just gave me a ring and proposed to me.

- Fred, your client from Aix-en-Provence?

- Yes, he asked me to move in with him. We have been seeing each other for more than a year, and in the last few months things were a little different between us. I felt the lack, the impatience to find him, I decided to accept.

- *Mazal tov*, Pretty Woman!

We keep in touch, her new status as a young fiancée does not make me unattractive. When I go down to Nice, we have lunch together. I stop in Aix-en-Provence, meet her in her new residence and tell her about the indecency of the huge diamond that is now on her finger.

So far, I have never had a crush on a client. I have found some very sexy, interesting ones, some I could have hit on in my everyday life or others I have seen again, just for fun.

I have for example Chris, a guy from Nice who is not much older than me and who, since we met, sends me daily messages to check up on me, to wish me a nice day or a sweet night. He has the perfect resume of the ideal boyfriend and the way he tackles me against the wall when he arrives in the apartment amazes me. When you meet a man with whom there is a perfect sexual osmosis, orgasms are more valuable than euros. In order to enjoy his virility at my leisure, I don't charge him anymore, but I don't expect anything from him, his status as a lover is all I want to offer him. He seems perfect, but I want to be free.

There was also Stan who, as he was leaving, said to me:

"Mathilda, we're not going to pretend, we're not going to say see you soon, we know very well that we'll never see each other again."

I had spent an exceptional evening. The young man was great, brilliant, funny, handsome, a good lover with a good situation, and free of any commitment according to him. I felt like I was being dumped, we had been seducing each other throughout the evening. I wanted to see him again in another context and I lived it like a small disappointment in love, which lasted only fifteen minutes, the time of the return journey, but nevertheless.

There are also some whose way of life left me dreaming:

"I, Mathilda, am not rich, I am richest."

Leave me a Tip! No? The most affluent are not the most generous. I like to be offered a rose, a bouquet is too much, it has no place. A rose is elegant, sexy, suggestive almost naughty. Yes, there are men who, on their own initiative, go to a florist to buy me flowers. Incredibly, I have received more from my customers than from my lovers. Gifts too, boxes with beauty products, vouchers to enjoy treatments or boxes of chocolates, because :

"I don't think it's elegant to give you money hand over fist, I prefer pretty boxes."

But are these caring men also caring for their wives?

"Mathilda, what is happening between us is neither an insult nor a lack of respect to my wife, I simply need to escape from my daily life and my habits. It's a dose of youth and freshness that I inject myself with, a serum against weariness. And then, I'll be very honest, I'm tired of begging for a little affection. I imagine that my wife is lucid and that she accepts my pseudo-infidelities, because it suits her perfectly to delegate the conjugal duties."

Some of my colleagues think that we should be reimbursed by social security, for the good of couples, as an alternative to therapy. I think we are more like cosmetic surgery, a comfort treatment, not an antibiotic to cure a disease.

Normally they say: "No zob in job", but for me this rule does not count, so I never forbid myself during my meetings. A client could very well become a lover, but can an *escort* really become a lover?

Several of them offered it to me, but I had the feeling that they wanted to buy me. And I'm not one of those people who accept to "marry well", I believe too much in myself and in love for that. Others seemed really sincere and attached, but if they had met me in another context would they have been interested in me? In this context, I represent the free, independent, uninhibited woman, I am only a fantasy, a feminine ideal of which one dreams, but which in everyday life frightens most men.

14. As a professional sportswoman

In January 2014, I am in my apartment rented for a month in Nice. In the middle of the day, the city is plunged into darkness, a storm is coming from the sea. The waves of several meters high come down on the Promenade des Anglais. I observe from my window the palm trees which try to resist to the power of the wind, the streets are deserted. I've been here for three days and my phone doesn't ring, I'm walking in circles, taking stock of my life. Where am I at? It's been sixteen months since I left my job at the newspaper and almost two years since I started dating. I lie to myself that I am doing this to save money, to start a business. I don't have a project or a goal. Every euro I earn, I spend: hairdresser, extensions, false nails, beautician, handbags and shoes. I've become superficial, I'm always dressed up and only go to trendy places. I travel a little and enjoy life a lot without worrying about tomorrow. I party a lot, go to Paris often and make new friends that Elijah introduced to me. Girls who, when they are out, get paid if the young man wants to finish the evening with them. They don't have ads, they don't make a living from it, but they make ends meet when the opportunity arises.

I have not seen these two years pass. Time flies and I have hardly any personal lovers or the shadow of a lover. My lifestyle is not compatible with a couple relationship. And sex and money are no substitute for love and affection. This life of a party girl with no attachments no longer satisfies me.

I face the storm in Nice to go to a hairdresser's downstairs. I go in with Maryline Monroe's blond hair and leave with Carla Bruni's brown hair. It is said that when a woman changes her hair color, it is to change her life, I do not escape this stereotype. I pack my suitcase and, under a driving rain, I go back to Lyon. I took stock of the money I had saved, of the amount of my fixed expenses and of what I really needed to live. If I keep a few regulars, I can get by. If I find a job that doesn't pay too bad, I can quit. I update my resume and am determined to find a small temp job to get back into the swing of things gently, but with the goal of getting into an ambitious project in the near future and making room for love. I leave my ad online, but I don't answer any more requests for meetings, I lose the desire of ephemeral meetings. It is the passage of 30 years, the great questioning of decades. When I returned to Lyon, I went to Elijah's house, without taking the time to unpack my suitcase.

- Mathilde, you have the life you want and you are alone with yourself. No one will do things for you, my dear, and you are the only one to decide on your actions.

- I know, Elijah. When we came back from London over a year ago, I remember exactly what you said to me: "There are girls much trashier than you and they don't even charge for it. I know, I fuck them! You have nothing to be ashamed of, not everyone can understand it, hear it, but it's utopian to imagine that there are only coerced girls and fat people in this field. It may even be an opportunity for you, it can open doors, make you stronger, but don't forget that you are like a high level sportswoman, your career is short, you have to prepare the after, think about the future."

- It's true that I've fucked some really dirty ones!

- Elijah! That's the only thing you remember!

- Sweetie, you're a smart woman, I'm not worried about you.

As a professional athlete, it's time to look to the future. My biological clock tells me that eternal youth exists only in movies, that I am not Julia Roberts and that I am unlikely to meet Richard Gere. I received a message from Sandra, her fairy tale ended, as it often does in life. She kept the diamond, but saw her dreams vanish.

Living without a goal, without objectives or projects is only pleasant for a while. My thirst for entrepreneurship is no longer satisfied by the business stories told to me by men. I had the chance to meet great entrepreneurs, gentlemen who, during our meetings, drop the suit, speak without filter or speech previously written by a third party. I was fascinated by them, they made me grow, they passed on to me some of their knowledge, their thoughts: "If you don't know where you want to go, how can you know which path to take? Having goals is essential."

I aspire to be happy. It seems like an easy answer and it doesn't mean anything: "What makes you happy?"

I have a look at my messages and receive a request for services from a man who has been trying to meet me for several months, he regularly sends me SMS: "Hello, I am Franck, 42 years old, French Caucasian, brown, brown eyes, 1m73, quite thin, 63 kg and sport. I can receive you at my home in Chaponnay, 15 km from Lyon, thank you, looking forward to reading you, kiss."

I accept, because the transition of my life is underway, my journey is beginning. I don't have any job offers from temp agencies yet and I have to anticipate the future financially.

We have an appointment at 7:30 pm. On the way, I receive a first message.

- Do you want to take a shower?

- No, I'm getting out of it, but if you want to have one together, no problem.

I don't like it, showers are very erotic, sensual, you have to get naked. I don't have any more panties or stockings, no more artifices, I am vulnerable. I am not Mathilda, I am Mathilde, and I don't want to be Mathilde at every meeting. Some are insipid, to some men I don't offer languorous kisses nor greedy preliminaries, just doggy style with badly played moans.

- It's up to you, mine is from this morning at 7:30. It's to see if I heat the bathroom.

But where will I fall? How can you bring an *escort* and not take a shower? Normally, I am a gift, the Christmas Eve feast, and all the decor should match this little moment that you give yourself and enjoy almost exclusively. How can you plan to have an intimate relationship without being perfectly *clean*?

- I invite you to freshen up, since 7:30 this morning... I'll be there in 15 minutes, enjoy.

- Together then?

- If not, you enjoy it until I get there.

- Would you rather I freshen up first or with you?

I don't answer, what doesn't he understand in: "You enjoy it before I arrive"? I know what he wants from me, but I don't get ahead of myself. If, during our moral contract on the phone, a man doesn't express a wish for a service, I'm not obliged to do anything and if he puts me to the wall, I'll know how to get out of it. It is always a bad sign to receive a multitude of messages before I arrive. A gentleman doesn't do that, he validates our agreement by phone, everything is said and clear. He sends me a message a few hours before our meeting to make sure I'm not doing him wrong, then he waits, pines, prepares and looks good. He doesn't pester me with stupid questions.

- You want me to be clean?

No, I prefer if you stink of piss.

Already not very enthusiastic these last weeks about the idea of meeting people, I arrive tense at the indicated address. It is a subdivision. Yellow plaster walls and a dilapidated wooden gate surround the duplex house. I look over the gate, it is behind the French window. Next to him is a large, long-haired dog.

- Don't worry, she's not mean.

Yes, I do. All the things I hate are combined in one date. I don't care much for men's looks, up to a point. If there's one thing that's a deal breaker for me, it's teeth. He has an ashtray in his mouth and a skinny little *geek* body. He wears jeans that are too wide, a cotton jogging jacket and plaid charentaises with holes. He welcomes me in slippers with holes in them, I find that scandalous! Seduction is not only one way during these meetings, and if he receives me in such a sloppy way, he must not consider me much.

I enter the house, he brings out the dog, I tell him I am afraid of it. The room is big, but the floor is covered with hair, paw prints, the smell is nauseating and there is a mess everywhere. There is a pile of clothes on every chair and armchair, dusty knick-knacks on every piece of furniture, and papers littering the various sideboards. My home is very uncluttered, I like the "model home" feel. Everything has a place, every cushion is correctly aligned, nothing is lying around. Living in a multitude of bric-a-brac, I find it distressing.

I instantly go into *acting* mode, and even though he is rather pleasant and friendly, I don't feel like being interested in him, and I find it hard to pretend. The lack of prestige of the place reminds me that everything is not only glitter. He offers me a coffee, I ask him to serve me a long one, to pass the time. He didn't take a shower, not knowing if I wanted to take it with him. I dodge and invite him to do it during my coffee. He asks me to go with him to the bathroom to talk, he has already paid me and only wants to watch me, I know it. We go upstairs, there are three children's rooms.

- Are you sure you don't want to shower with me? There's a bathtub or shower that's small, but we'll be close together and if you come with me you can make sure I'm clean. On the other hand, if you don't come with me you'll be able to watch me naked while I soak.

I don't watch it. I'm not interested in seeing him naked, I'm on the show *It's Clean*. The bathroom is as cluttered as the other rooms in the house, there are products everywhere. He washes himself while telling me banalities, I don't listen to him, I sketch : "Hum hum, yes, yes". The parental room is on the first floor. The

married men who welcome me in their home have the decency
not to invite me in the bed of madam, but on the sofa. He drags
me into the conjugal room. Like the rest of the house, his wife's
panties are lying on the floor, the clothes are in piles on all sides,
the bedside tables are covered with an inch of dust, and on the
dressing room door is stuck with Patafix an *OK Podium* poster of
Patrick Bruel. It must be a stimulus for his wife, at this moment,
I understand her: "Patrickkkk, come and save me!"

He starts to kiss me, I pinch my lips. He tries to force his tongue
into my mouth, I don't let him, I squeeze my lips even harder.
He smells cold tobacco, alcohol and had to drink to relax before
my arrival. He would have done better to wash and tidy up or
to offer a cleaning lady to his wife instead of paying an *escort*.
He asks me to take off my stockings, he prefers the contact of
the skin. No, I don't want to get naked on this bed, to be against
him, I can live with doggy style, but not body to body. I do it
anyway, I can't deny him everything. This is part of the disadvantages, sometimes the man displeases me. I could have left
when I arrived, but as in any activity, there are times when you
have to take it easy. A nurse doesn't like to do all the nursing, a
cook doesn't like all the food she cooks, and a secretary doesn't
want to get up every morning to put up with her colleagues and
see her boss's face.

He asks me for a 69, I know I have a card to play. A good
blowjob is just technique like a recipe. First of all, lick the
penis from bottom to top to moisten it and arouse the desire.
Secondly, insert the glans and then the whole member into the
oral cavity. Exercise rather slow back and forth movements by
affixing the lips. Add a hand that jerks up and down, but also in a

14. As a professional sportswoman

circular way while continuing the oral introduction. Sprinkle the whole of some strokes of tongue by varying the cadence: slow, fast. Squeeze the penis more or less hard. Break the rhythm to accentuate the peak of pleasure. Not to let settle a lassitude, it is the principal ingredient so that this recipe is successful. Then, to finish, with the second hand knead the testicles. This requires indeed a certain coordination and dexterity of the movements, it is necessary to use at the same time its mouth, its lips, its tongue and its two hands. Not easy without training, I grant you! But, in less than three minutes, he asks me to stop. He tries to control himself, serves his glans between his fingers, but can't stop himself from ejaculating.

He is embarrassed and apologizes, "I was too excited."

It's made for.

There are rules in my field, one ejaculation per hour of appointment, otherwise you have to pay extra, we call it an *extra ball*. Therefore, my physical performance is over. I am in no way responsible for his premature ejaculation and his lack of *self-control*. I doubt that he knows the collective agreement of the prostitutes, but no one is supposed to ignore the laws, even if they don't really exist.

He goes up to shower, I take advantage of it to get dressed completely. There are still thirty minutes left on the clock, my objective now is to make him talk, in twenty minutes I can leave. I don't want him to bring up the subject of a second round, even with an extra charge, I don't want to do it. He comes back in his robe, surprised that I've already put it on. I know the owners are passionate about their pets, so I bring up the subject of the dog, the breed, the kibble. He gives me the history of the family companions, even the dead ones. The clock is ticking and to sound the final gong:

- What will you do next?

- Is it time already? It's a shame, we spent the whole time talking.

It was already too much for me. My clothes are covered in hair and I smell like a wet dog. I put everything in the machine and ran to the shower when I got home. He wasn't mean to me, he was even accommodating. I almost stole from him by giving him such a poor performance. I feel bad about it, but I tell myself that I have come to the end of the experience.

15. Champagne!

In April 2014, a few days before my 30th birthday and after two years of prostitution, I delete my online ad and throw away the chip from my work phone. Without a word, without goodbye or farewell. My regular clients must have heard one day: the number you have dialed is no longer assigned. For those who have my personal contact information and with whom I have developed friendly ties, we do not break contact, my "retirement" does not put an end to our good relationship.

I landed a three-month assignment for an online job platform. I work with four field salesmen, for whom I make estimates, invoices, customer follow-ups, and check the conformity of the ads.

- Hello, my little mother, I work on Monday!

- Are you working on Monday?

- Yes, I found a temporary job.

- That's good news, my daughter, even if I would have preferred a permanent contract, but after two years of doing nothing, I think I'll be happy with it.

- Are you looking for a permanent contract?

- Stop your nonsense, you know very well what I mean. In any case, it's one less thing to worry about, it's not a life of doing nothing.

- But I don't do nothing, I live, and living my little mama takes time!

I arrive in this *open space* in Vaise, completely lost, out of phase and out of place. I went from being a prostitute to a sales assistant in the space of a month. Even if I have worked more often in an office than on the sidewalk, this two-year interlude is not insignificant. I am no longer the same person, I no longer obey the rules. I feel like a starlet forced to return to work after failing in show business. However, I have developed a great ability to adapt. I assimilate quickly and am quickly efficient in the missions that I am entrusted with. I carry them out with professionalism, but my way of being, my exuberance and my apparent "I don't care" disconcert my colleagues. I have become an alien in the world of work, not a model employee who tries to look good to get a permanent contract. I am in transition, trying to readjust, to get back into a rhythm of life, to have constraints, office hours, to prepare a Tupperware and to eat in the small kitchen with the co-workers with a tidy life. I'm the laughing stock, the bad student who arrives perched on 12 cm Louboutin heels and contradicts the sales manager without restraint. My superiors understand that I am unfiltered and use it to transfer all the calls from unhappy customers to me.

"Mr. Dumont, you hold our platform responsible for the lack of candidates for your ad. You are trying to recruit a mechanical engineer with 4 years of higher education, trilingual in German and English, to work in the export market. You offer an employee status and a salary of 30K per year. In all objectivity, don't you think, Mr. Dumont, that the lack of candidates is due to the mediocrity of the offer and the working conditions?"

Mr. Dumont became my best friend during my mission, and even though he was always unhappy, he passed on all his job offers to me, sometimes improving the terms of the contract.

I enjoy getting up every morning. This is my new playground, I have a desk, Post-it notes, a chair with wheels, a double computer screen and a headset to make calls. I'm having fun, but I'm turning down the offer of a job at the end of the assignment.

- But why?

- I've been here for three months, I've been around, I'm bored. Quotes, ads, it was nice to meet you, but I want something else.

I am failing almost miserably in this attempt to reintegrate. But I think that every step in life leads to something or someone. I leave this interim mission with a new friend, Cécile de Florançon, from the Parisian nobility. She calls her grandmother "vous" and addresses her as "bonne maman". She grew up in mansions and her father drove her to school in a Ferrari. Our life paths are diametrically opposed, but we share more important values than that, open-mindedness and curiosity. One day she asks me:

- Before working here, what did you do? Because you have an atypical personality, you know that, Mathilde? You are not like everyone else!

- Escort.

- Really? When we were 10-12 years old, Dad took my sister and me to rue Saint-Denis in Paris. It was the middle of the afternoon. We walked along the sidewalk and he explained to us what

15. Champagne!

prostitution was. He told us to always respect these women and that the world would be a worse place if they were not there. That he didn't wish this on us as a future, but that courtesans have always been part of the court.

- I was not born at the right time, my Cecile!

In July 2014, at the end of my temping contract, a friend of Elijah's informs me that an atmospheric bar-restaurant is looking for girls to host the establishment.

- A champagne bar?

- This is not a classic champagne bar. It's a restaurant with home-made food. The guys from the construction industry come here for lunch, there are also cops and politicians. They meet to sign contracts, to please their clients. In the evening, there are theme parties and the girls put on the atmosphere, dance, sing, but there is no sex.

I'm running because getting paid to party is like being a mystery shopper for luxury hotels, it's enticing. I'm far from the goal I set at the beginning of the year, to resume a career and evolve, but first things first.

It is 3 pm when I arrive in this discreet street of Villeurbanne. About ten customers are on the terrace, four young women are chatting with them. I enter, it's a charming restaurant, unpretentious but warm. The owner is behind the bar, a flamboyant redhead, 50 years old, with a glass of champagne in her hand and a plunging neckline on her voluptuous chest. She offers me a friendly welcome and hands me a flute full of bubbles. About fifteen customers inside are finishing their lunch, chatting, laughing in the company of five girls dressed in summer dresses. It's reassuring, I already went to have a drink with friends in a champagne bar, the ladies were all in lingerie and the atmosphere was creepy. Here, it is not the case. Laurence, the owner, invites me to follow her into the back room equipped with disco balls, a video and hifi system, microphones for karaoke nights and a bar that runs the length of the room.

"Here, it's simple Mathilde, we party. Most of the customers are regulars, friends. They come to have fun, to relax and they like to be accompanied by nice girls. You like to party, you like alcohol, do you want to be paid for it? I'll give you an extra contract as a waitress at the minimum wage, because you'll also have to serve, but you'll also get a variable part, you'll get 30% of what you consume. If a customer offers you a glass of champagne, I sell it for 20 euros, you get 6 euros back, and the same goes for the bottles. You can come to work during the day or in the evening and you choose the days you are present. Do you want to try the adventure?

To talk with men, I have the necessary skills and experience, to party, I have a bachelor's degree for that, to work when I want, it is exactly what I need. I decide to work daytime hours, Monday to Friday. I have to arrive at 11:30 am for the lunch service, and I leave when I want depending on the number of customers.

- Marina, I was going to call you, I found a new job.

- We were talking about it, I'm with mom. What are you going to do?

- Waitress in a festive restaurant.

- My daughter, in restaurant and festive, where is the word work?

- In waitress! Waitress, it's a job, right? So, we might as well do it in a good mood, right?

- But, it's a champagne bar? my sister Marina retorts to me with an appalled look.

- No, it's a restaurant. So there is champagne like in all restaurants, but I have to do the service and the animation, a bit like G.O. at Club Med.

I start the next day. We are about ten girls who take turns, most of them are in their twenties, students or unemployed, of all origins, and all extremely friendly. I am the new girl, the attraction of the assembly. I am offered glasses by all the customers who are, indeed, for the majority of the company managers in the building industry. It is an atmosphere of "bouchon lyonnais", we eat mom's cooking, drink red wine, as an appetizer we are served sausage and pie. We are among friends, there is some flirting and some jokes, nothing scary. But, even if I can hold my liquor pretty well, I go home at night a little tipsy, I drink more than twenty glasses a day. I do an hour of sport every morning to allow my body to evacuate and try to keep a certain hygiene of life. After a week, I know all the regulars and sing at the top of my lungs with the other girls when the anthem of the bar and of the moment rings out: "Party girls don't get hurt, Can't feel anything, When will I learn, One, Two, Three Drink"[4].

In French: "Les filles fêtardes ne souffrent jamais, Elles sont tellement insensibles, Quand deviendrai-je comme elles... One, Two, Three drinks".

It's like *Coyote Girls,* we put on a show, dress up, hold Miss and Mister elections, have bocce contests in the square next door, play 421 and smoke inside. We are paid to have fun and to spread

---

4. Sia, *Chandelier.*

a festive atmosphere. Every man, or woman, because we also have female customers, knows when they arrive, but never when they leave. This is the kind of place that makes you lose track of time. You can arrive at noon and leave at midnight, without even realizing it. At a certain time, the door of the restaurant closes, the owner pulls the heavy black curtains in front of the windows, blocking any view of the outside world, and time stops for the champagne to flow.

No customer has ever offered me to do an "extra" and none of the girls have mentioned it. However, in the eyes of the *average* passer-by, we are classified and listed as a hooker bar. A bar of atmosphere, it is inevitably a bar with whores.

"Mathilde, honey, this place is going to be my H.Q. The buddies from London are coming next week, I know where I'm taking them!"

I quickly feel at ease in this restaurant, I have fun with my colleagues who all seem satisfied to be paid to party. I sympathize with the customers who are only looking for a break in their often busy schedule.

16. An evidence

Two weeks after my arrival, I hire in the late morning, ready to feast again. The restaurant is still almost empty, I am the first of the girls present. I am the one who leaves early in the evening and arrives early in the morning, if we can say that noon is early in the morning! As is customary, I greet the customers, kiss those I know and introduce myself to those I have never seen before. A single man is sitting at the bar. I approach him. He is wearing a navy blue suit jacket, very elegant and fitted, over a white shirt with small lilac-blue field flowers, matched with dark jeans and a pair of camel-colored dress shoes. His head is shaved, his complexion tanned, his teeth are white and perfectly aligned. In spite of the years, fifty certainly passed, his face is not marked, his glance is at the same time cold and laughing, his left eyebrow forms a circumflex accent and it is for half white. He takes large puffs on his cigarette while sipping a glass of rosé. He greets me politely, without lingering. I sit down beside him, intrigued by his behavior. He is there, alone, doesn't talk to anyone, doesn't read the newspaper and doesn't even look at his phone.

- Hello, my name is Mathilde, can I sit with you?

- Yes, please, do you want something to drink?

- The same as you, a rosé, but in the pool. Are you waiting for someone?

- I never wait for anyone, Miss.

Lolo, the owner, brings me my drink.

- Nico, let me introduce you to Mathilde, my new recruit. I'm sure you'll like her. Mathilde, be careful, Nico is not just any customer, he's like my brother.

I grab my glass to toast with him and, in a hurry, half spill it on his beautiful flowered shirt.

- A clumsy one, that starts well! And it's the first drink!

It takes me a moment to lose my temper and not want to leave him. We have several drinks together without him telling me anything about himself. He keeps me talking, interested in me, my background, my family, my passions, why I work here. I don't talk about my activity of the last two years, it is not part of my life anymore. It's not necessary to talk about this with a complete stranger, but I give myself up by playing the charmer. When he leaves the restaurant, a customer calls out to me: "Are you hanging out with the cops?"

He comes back the next day, I am already installed with a group of customers. I finish my drink quickly and come to settle down beside him. I find him handsome, charismatic, classy and mysterious. After two years of dating a lot of mature men, age is no longer a problem for me, it's even the opposite, time makes a man desirable.

- Are you reading me my rights today, before you start your interrogation like yesterday?

- Clever girl, I notice that you've been asking around.

- I didn't have to, the information just came to me. Unfriendly people are often put to death by those who want to be like them!

- I'm not a cop anymore, I'm retired.

- So young! How good it is to be a civil servant!

- Insolent!

A former bodyguard of celebrities, he was part of the close protection of political figures, religious figures and major world stars before joining the police force. He's a movie cop, a leading man in Olivier Marchal's films, the kind of cop who gives you the impression of being a thug, but who doesn't accept baksheesh or deals. He's a freemason, a lover of pétanque, mechanics, binge drinking and pretty women, especially if they are African, which is not lacking here. But at this moment, it is me that he devours with his eyes, it is for me now that he comes every day to have a glass of rosé, between two meetings for an organization of which he is the president in Lyon.

The day after our meeting, he suggested that I meet him at the end of my shift for a game of pétanque at the Café de la Mairie, quai Pierre-Scize in the 9e district of Lyon. I joined him with my heart beating wildly, I pointed masterfully, we won and Cupid launched his arrow.

He becomes my lover, my lover, I see in him the man of my life.

- Marina, I think I met someone.

- What do you mean, sister?

- I think it's him. How do we know it's him?

- We don't know, it's obvious!

- It's obvious, in my heart it's obvious, but he's older than me.

- So what? I am four years older than my husband and that doesn't stop me from being pregnant with my second child.

16. An evidence

- Yes, but he is much older than me.

- Is he dead? No, so if he's still alive and well, isn't that the important thing?

An instantaneous love at first sight. We are twenty-five years apart, but I am completely in love with him. We live a passionate and fusional love story. I find him every evening, leave my service early to be with him. And I have trouble with alcohol on a daily basis, I have nightmares and my nights are very restless. I wake up in the morning sweating and having been murdered three times during the night. I cut back on my shifts and only go to restaurants when he is not available to spend time with me. He takes me to receptions at the prefecture, introduces me to his friends, who are astonished to see him on the arm of a white woman, he who is so fond of mixed race.

- It's nice to see Nico with a girl like you, you have class, conversation, you're not just a bimbo with green lenses, a wig and a big ass.

- It's disturbing, reductive and fascist what you are telling me.

- Fascist, right now! It's genetic! Blacks have big asses, besides you are a bit African, aren't you? You have to do the same things to her as the black girls, but on top of that, you go through the motions in the social evenings. You look like Clothilde de Courau, dirty, but Clothilde de Courau!

- Florent, not that I'm rigid and frigid, but every other sentence you utter is inappropriate.

- I'm kidding, but how did he get you to jump, he made you think he had money?

- Why, did you see a price tag on me? I'm lucky to be with him, I could have fallen for a man like you.

Being in the arms of an older man gives others permission to treat you like a venal, self-serving whore looking for her own father. It's the Oedipus complex, you've got to have something to settle or a bill to pay.

For me to like a man, I have to admire him. An amateur chef capable of playing with knives like Christian Têtedoie, a worker who is passionate about the constellations and knows the name of each of the stars, or a Sunday sportsman who is preparing for the SaintéLyon, I have to be subjugated to like him.

Nico fascinates me with his aura, his presence. He dominates me, channels me. After two years of prostitution, I feel for the first time the desire to give myself to someone, to vibrate. I am no longer a prostitute who gets wet on command, I am a woman who makes love because she loves.

- Your eyes are sparkling, Mathilde.

- I'm in love, Aurore, can you believe it?

- It happens even to the most resistant! You just had to let your guard down, but stay alert, I'm not going to teach you how men are.

Nico makes me discover a Lyon I don't know, which is reserved only for the big guys of the city, only on invitation card. He abandons me in the crowd, harassed by people I don't know and finds me in the company of the prefect's wife who only has eyes for me: "Your friend is divine, Nicolas".

I am divine, fabulous, almost the first lady in this Lyon microcosm. I am nothing and nobody, only "the new girl" in their parties in need of gossip. I don't have a membership card and I am not fooled. But I play them like they play me. If the prefect's wife knew that six months ago I was walking the corridors of the

16. An evidence

hotels of Nice, I am not sure that the adjective "divine" would have come to her mind. But it's a lot of fun to go from these two extremes of life to the other. It has always driven me, to be everything and its opposite, to reinvent myself, to multiply projects, the need for novelty, to discover, to learn and to know. Not to remain confined in a classic and predefined scheme. To be where I am not expected and where I myself had not imagined. The greatest pleasure I took during my appointments was to feed myself with the knowledge of the men. I was able to infiltrate their companies, their sectors of activity, their sciences and discover so many different environments. Often, people say to me, "But, Mathilde, how do you know that? Where did you learn all this?"

I have acquired skills and knowledge in hotel rooms, as a continuing education in a professional environment.

One evening, with Nico, we discuss honesty, loyalty and trust.

- Trust does not preclude control, he tells me. One evening, I walked my previous fiancée home. I waited downstairs, thinking she was in a bit of a hurry to get home. A few moments later, she came out, a man was waiting for her. She got into her car. I investigated and discovered that she was an *escort*.

One more, I'm not surprised anymore.

- That doesn't make her a bad girl.

- No, but my status does not allow me to endorse it. She was doing it while we were together, that's treason. I don't wish anyone to find out that their girlfriend is a whore.

I hope not to be listed on any police file, I don't want to become this "yet another one". I am aware that few men can accept this parenthesis of my life, this modern libertarianism, this sexual trend that I have chosen to experiment with. To have too many lovers is to have too much power, too many points of comparison. It is not humiliating for a woman, it is offensive for a man. It is directly reaching his primary instinct of dominance, it puts him in a position of weakness, therefore uncomfortable.

Weeks go by without any suspicion to darken our romance, but as the saying goes, love stories usually end badly, and ours is no exception.

Trust does not exclude control, he told me. It's the kind of sentence that stays with me. I see his car several times parked near the girls' restaurant. I don't work there anymore, I'm looking for a new job again. Nico gave me the opportunity to meet the president of an employers' confederation, I sent him my CV and I am waiting for an interview, so I have time. One day, I waited several hours, hidden in an alley adjacent to the restaurant. I am one of those women, when I have a doubt, I raise it, elaborate a strategy, spy and try to be smarter.

I see him out with one of my former colleagues, he wraps his arm around her hips and embraces her languidly. His desire for African women has caught up with him. I am devastated, and as a wounded woman I write to him: "How can you do this to me? What is she doing to you that I am not doing to you? I thought you loved me."

We do not hold men by sex, in any case, it is not enough to make them faithful.

I don't forgive him, I have the image of this girl in front of my eyes. Knowing is hard, but seeing is even worse.

I am a whore and will be a whore all my life. It's like a tattoo embedded in me. The day of my first pass, I became a whore and, like a president, it's for life. But, that's also true for everything.

16. An evidence

If you've been a hairdresser and you're retooling, you're still a hairdresser, but you're not practicing anymore. The use of the word "whore" is shocking, it irritates the ears and sounds like a swear word, an insult.

- Don't say whore, Mathilde, you are not a whore, you are an *escort*, a courtesan.

- Yes, well, Cécile, I have never seen much difference. My art and I don't need to be ennobled. I know that in your "particle" world, the title is important, but in my world, only the values really count.

I am used to unfaithful men, to the dissociation between body and heart, between sex and love, but in my personal life I don't accept it, don't want to see it or know it. Cheat on me one night, get drunk, abandon yourself in the sheets of a beautiful stranger, satisfy your animal urges with a girl who agrees to it, but never maintain a relationship, never have a regular mistress, never strut in the arms of another and always arrange so that I never discover your infidelities. I'm experiencing real heartache, scarring my arms to keep from getting to my wrists. And I am learning the hard way that we cannot accept everything. Forgiveness has no place in passion. You have to be reasonable to be able to forgive. I am not reasonable. I have never been reasonable.

17. Positive thinking

October 2014. A year ago, I would have gone to Nice with a flourish and a light spirit. Today, I'm sitting on the back of my couch, with a bag of chips and a chocolate bar, with an inert look and greasy hair. I am starting to write a book entitled: *Love is shit.* Then I tell myself that being pessimistic has never made anyone happy. There are people who never encounter a single obstacle in their lives, for whom everything seems easy and beautifully written. Women who go from a beautiful story to a wonderful one, from an exciting job to a promising career. And there are those like me who, at every intersection, must redouble their efforts to avoid being swept away by a mudslide and succeed at all costs in not sinking into the current. But isn't that what is so exciting? To start over, to fight, to take control of your fears and to kick your daily life to the curb because no, love is not shit and life is not rotten. I took what was there to take, when the universe gave it to me. I have experienced unforgettable moments, thrills so powerful that they froze my blood, heartbeats so strong that my chest could have exploded. These emotions, no one will be able to take them away from me, steal them from me and make me forget them. So yes, once again, I am alone with myself and my most faithful friend, disillusionment. But, it is not a fatality, it is only an obstacle that is insurmountable if you do not believe in yourself. I often think of some lines I read in a poetry book in my early teens:

"Let the days, the months, the years go by, wherever you are, whatever you do, when you think you've hit rock bottom, never forget that I'm here.

Over time, I took on the interpretation of these writings and decided that the author was speaking to himself. For we are our own weaknesses, but above all we are our own strength, and our fighting spirit can only come from deep within. Tomorrow is another day, and if you think hard enough that the best is yet to come, then fate will hear you.

I end 2014 by redoubling my efforts every morning at the gym and doing a few small assignments: salesperson for a Lyon radio station, assistant in an industry. Applying obsolete processes that have no meaning or interest, but were designed to remind employees that they must follow, like a horse with its blinders, the path without ever deviating in order to stay in the right box.

- Mathilde, you are not on the steering committee. We give you procedures to follow, whether you think they are good or not is not the point. We just expect you to follow them.

- But, if I'm being proactive and my reasoning is logical, maybe you could review these procedures and make them evolve, for the good of your company and your employees?

- If we wanted an audit, we would have called in a professional. You are an assistant and, again, Mathilde, you are not on the executive committee. Do as you are told or take your business.

- Can I take Post-it notes with me? To plaster my fridge with this benevolent advice: "Do as you're told Mathilde". Maybe it will eventually fit?

To submit to a tidy life devoid of meaning and interest is the opposite of my personality. Tolerating and resigning myself to being nothing but a robot whose every action and thought is dictated to me cannot make me happy.

- My daughter, you can't live outside the box all the time, think about your retirement.

- My retirement? Dad died ten years before he could enjoy his. Do you think that if someone had told him at the age of 30: "Man, you're going to work hard all your life and at 55 you're going to die", you don't think he would have told you: "Mina, now is the time to live, come on, we're taking risks, we don't care about owning property, we don't care about working for a miserable salary. Pour yourself a rosé Mina, take a sheet of paper, a pen and make a list of your desires".

There are people who, all their life, are complacent in a job, in a mediocre and unsatisfactory life as a couple, because it is much easier to live with what we have, to complain, than to turn a situation around. To change is risky, but to stagnate is to die.

- Mathilde, but you have this strength.

- I don't have a choice, Aurore, and you do the same, you take classes at the university, you are on call at the hospital. Your parents can't help you financially and you don't come from a family of doctors. Yet you are in your sixth year of medical school now, thanks to your motivation. Your weeks are 80 hours long and you don't even earn minimum wage. You are much stronger than me and I am so proud of you.

Positive thinking is not a concept, but a way of life in my opinion.

During a dinner with friends, I met Tom: "Mathilde, I'm opening a restaurant in the Monts d'Or. If you're free, I'm looking for a barmaid to help me some evenings and weekends."

I prefer the lightheartedness of a bar counter to the rigidity of a computer keyboard, so he doesn't have to do much to recruit me.

Tom is a real character, a man of the night who has turned his passion for partying into a job by managing various nightclubs. His fair complexion suggests that the sun's rays don't often have the opportunity to feast on his skin, but his laughing eyes and large almond-shaped eyes are enough to illuminate his almost childlike face. Twenty-eight years old, ten of which have been masterfully orchestrating Lyon's festivities. He is a *showman* at heart. He imitates Céline Dion like no one else, always has the right joke at the right time, he is a joke *sniper*. I spend entire nights, when the curtain of the restaurant falls, almost peeing on myself while watching him perform. The attitudes, the mimics, the accents, he grabs a bottle in passing as a microphone and there he is *moonwalking* me in passing to make me twirl and then abandoning me on a chair: "Don't try to steal the show, I'm the artist!"

Tom knows my old life perfectly well, but we never talk about it: "Mathilde, it's not you, you know that very well."

Is it not me? And why wouldn't it be me? Very often, when my status as an *escort comes up in* conversation, my interlocutors tell me that: "You don't look like one". As if there was a particular sign that distinguishes prostitutes or that my Stan Smiths and my eloquence were a bulwark against this activity. We are beings, not identical inflatable dolls made on a production line.

- Did you wear red wigs and false eyelashes?

- I am not a transformist! A little artist, but in *working girl* mode, pencil skirt and pumps. No feathers or boa!

There is also a remark that I can't stand and that holds the prize for hypocrisy: "I thought you were being maintained by an old rich man or, at worst, that you were cheating on guys. Now you don't really realize, selling your body…"

If cheating is more acceptable, I am really worried about the future of our society. If stealing, lying, manipulating and playing with others seems more acceptable than an honest agreement between two parties, it is time to review the definitions of "respect" and "respectable".

18. BE WHAT THE COMPANY WANTS

After six interviews, and after having memorized the new decrees of the Macron and Hamon laws, the functioning of the "compte pénibilité" and all the governmental measures in force for very small businesses, the General Secretary of the Employers' Confederation, whom Nico, my lover, had given me the opportunity to meet, validated my recruitment to the position of External Relations Officer.

It is March 2015, I have not been a prostitute for a year. I now work for the most serious organization in town. The perfect big gap. I drink my coffee in front of BFM Business, read the economic press, follow the new start-ups closely. My mission is to recruit business leaders to join the confederation and accompany them in their entrepreneurial problems. I deal with the same clientele, my recruitment process is similar and my working method is almost identical to my *escort* method, but there is no sex. I have a free agenda, my hours, my office is at home. I have business objectives and I implement as I see fit my actions to achieve them. I open a Facebook page, a Twitter account and LinkedIn to canvass my future members. I schedule my meetings in cafés instead of hotels and sign contracts easily. The reputation of the confederation opens the door and my relational ease does the rest. I have business lunches and dinners, I participate in seminars, I am closer to the decision makers in Lyon and I blossom intellectually again in a profession. I no longer live my clients' lives through meetings, it has become my own.

I make a decent living, but to make ends meet I work as a waitress in my friend Tom's restaurant. I have one job during the week, another on the weekends, and every other day at 7:00 a.m. I work out with a private trainer whom I pay through extras, because I have no savings. One year after the beginning of my "retirement", I have nothing left. The money I earned, I spent to please myself, but also to benefit the people I love. I'm the one who pays the bill when you go to the bathroom in restaurants, who arrives at cocktail parties with my arms full, who fills up your car because you lent it to me to drive ten kilometers, who disguises the price of the vacation rental so that it doesn't cost you too much. I make you believe in a promotion and we end up at the Mamounia in Marrakech for 500 € a week *all inclusive*, flight included. I always like to share the good things in life.

When I stopped *escorting*, I divided my income very sharply, so I changed my lifestyle. I still have some habits, but my bling-bling period is over. I like beautiful and good things, but I am not superficial. Fake hair and nails are not for me. I'm not interested in hardware, I don't enjoy shopping and I don't have a great sense of fashion. I have a weakness for mechanics and high gastronomy, but if I like money, because I am not ashamed to say it and I do not find it vulgar, it is for the freedom it brings. Everything is possible, feasible and achievable. I have never been able to stand deprivation, maybe it's a consequence of too much dieting!

I feel like this new job is the opportunity of a lifetime. I am becoming an honorable person in the eyes of society, and joining this institution will give me opportunities. I only rub shoulders with business leaders, politicians, and *business angels*, and I'm not there to take care of them for an hour. I dream of being a startup, a partner, a businesswoman. I know all about the city's latest entrepreneurs and the latest business stars to come out of EM Lyon. I want to invest in every innovation that I discover and that fascinates me. I love my new job, my life, the people I work for, and I'm proud of my social ascension. I, the little country girl who started from nothing and went through almost everything, managed to climb the ladder until I became part of the "elite" of the city of Lyon.

During events like the "Soirée des Entrepreneurs", I meet familiar faces, looks that are too insistent to be the result of a heavy flirtation from a distance, smiles, winks or "I'm not sure":

- We've met before, haven't we?

- Lyon is a village! Perhaps you were present at the last confederation party?

Knowing how to bounce back, not letting yourself be destabilized. If people don't tell me things clearly, I play dumb. And I'm not afraid of being recognized, of being labeled a "whore," because I've never felt like I was doing anything wrong, unhealthy or degrading. I never thought, "If I do this, I won't be able to do anything, I'll be condemned to the margins of society.

18. Be what the company wants

No more social life, legal job or official lover." No! For me, I was an *escort girl*, as I was a saleswoman in a bakery, a cashier at Auchan, a saleswoman at Xerox, a temp agency manager, an assistant manager in the nuclear industry and so on, my CV is two pages long. Unstable for some recruiters, adaptable for others. For me, it is a line like any other, a path in my life, an experience, a way of life. And I never imagined that for others, it could be different. People who know me know what kind of person I am, those who don't know me don't know. And even if I did, what difference does it make? I rented my time to men to get us out of our loneliness, now I sell them memberships so they are no longer isolated in their entrepreneurial journey. We all have something to buy and sell and let's place our cursor on the scale of morality.

Being out of the box makes you a special specimen that some people would like to put down. When I arrived at the confederation, my female colleagues were very angry with me, because during my official presentation at a meeting, I said that I was not married and had no children. This was an affront to them, who translated this into: "I am hot and ready to suck to succeed".

Finally, you don't really have to be a prostitute to be one in the eyes of others, you just have to be older than the age of the cathe-rinettes, to be a little pretty and feminine. The higher your heels are, the higher you climb on the podium of the "puterie". And if your arrogance shows under your aplomb, then you're screwed.

"You know, Mathilde, I tell the office that I have a boyfriend. I made up a story, so they don't bother me. I avoid the questions, the "She must have a problem, she's over 30". So I stay away from the dating scene and people take you more seriously when you have someone in your life. Otherwise, you're either the old maid or the hottie in the club." This friend of Aurore's had come up with a defense that had never occurred to me. Be what society wants you to be to keep you out of trouble. Adapt and fit in rather than trying to change attitudes.

19. The crash of the century

On April 25, 2015, my birthday, I received a message from the confederation on my professional Facebook:

- Hello, it's not every day you turn 30, I offer you a helicopter flight.

- Hello, that's very kind, but I'm 31 years old today. Besides, I have already made a first flight in a helicopter, I pass.

- Have you ever flown at night over Lyon? In a plane? I am also a pilot.

I joined the confederation less than two months ago, but I'm starting to get used to receiving invitations. For parties, business breakfasts or even by journalists who trade contacts with me. I try not to be too impressionable, my mother always told me: "All that glitters is not precious". I keep this in mind, but a night flight over Lyon is surely magical.

- What does it look like?

- I only have her Facebook, Aurore. Quite honestly, he's not my type. He looks a little nerdy and paunchy. He has green eyes, so obviously on a mixed race person it's appealing, but he's not very attractive!

- At worst, you do a plane ride, we don't ask you to marry her!

- Anyway, he warned me. He's 33, not married, doesn't want children and doesn't even want a serious relationship.

- So take advantage of what it offers you. You have nothing to lose.

- Life anyway! We are talking about a date on a plane.

- Because you, now, are afraid of losing your life? You are afraid that life will lose you, yes!

It's May 4, 2015, an orange Audi R8 arrives downstairs from my house. I'm wearing a long floral chiffon summer dress, a pair of beige pumps and a little white denim jacket. It's spring, but it's almost summery. It is 7:30 pm, the wind blows and opens the slit of my dress with each of my steps. He gets out of the car and leaves the driver's side door open. He is a small meter eighty with a too developed abdominal belt for a young man of 30 years. He doesn't really have a style of dress, he's wearing a white polo shirt on which is written in capital letters "G-Star Vintage". Indeed, the color of the brand initially red fades and turns to pink, we are well in the *vintage*. His straight cut jeans are way too wide for him and his closely shaved goatee, which draws a mustache and a collar under his jaw going up to his ears, gives him the look of coming straight from the 1980s.

I approach him:

- Shall I take the wheel?

- No! I got out to open the passenger side door for you.

- Too bad! I'm sure I can handle this little racer! Didn't you find a flashier color?

- I am a shareholder, among others, in a company that rents luxury cars. We always choose flashy models. I thought you'd like it.

- That's nice, if you don't ask me to split the cost at the end of the evening. I'd rather warn you, I can't afford to fly in a private plane or rent this type of vehicle.

We take the ring road which connects Gratte-ciel to Bron aviation. The engine sings, the horses scream at each acceleration. We overtake on the right, we brake hard in front of the fixed speed cameras, we accelerate again, I look at the speedometer: 110, 150, 180, 220. I like speed and motor sports, every year my dad took me to see stages of the wine rally. The adrenalin of the race, the squealing tires, the exhaust pipes that fart, I told my father: "Later, I will be a rally driver". And since then, I sometimes think I'm Fangio at the wheel of my DS and never remain insensitive to a man who masters driving.

In a few minutes, we arrive at the business airport. He punches in a code on the security gate and the door opens. I've flown on airliners before, but I'm not familiar with the world of private aviation. I have never had the opportunity to walk freely in the "backstage" of an airport. I am now strolling on the tarmac in high heels facing the control tower. Orange and white windsocks swirl in the wind around the facilities. The ground markings are so bright yellow that they seem to pop out of the asphalt like 3D elements. The grass around the runways is as green and neat as that of a soccer stadium, and the small planes and helicopters around the hangars are lined up next to each other in a perfect spacing. Everything seems rigorous and perfect.

I hear a deafening engine noise, turn my head to admire a private Cessna Citation CJ3 jet starting its take-off run. I barely have time to count the number of windows, that it has already taken off and becomes tiny in the immensity of the sky.

19. The crash of the century

- Don't dream, ours is much smaller! I reserved the Fox Delta Lima. Of course, it is behind all the others in the hangar.

At arm's length, he pushes the planes to allow ours to get through. After several maneuvers, he pulls out a Piper PA-28. It's a small four-seater, with a navy blue belly and low tail and wing tips. I have to climb on it to get inside, I take off my shoes, lest my stilettos pierce it. I climb on the right wing of the plane by holding on to the shoulder of my pilot. I am not very confident, he is a small zinc who seems to be older than me. I get into the cockpit, put on the headset, microphone and stay stunned in front of the instruments that I try to decipher.

We are now both on board the aircraft, I attach my safety harness while he gives me some instructions, then he continues:

- Bron, good morning, Fox Delta Lima, PA-28 at the parking club. Let's ask for a local flight with A information.

- Fox Delta Lima, hello, call back for the ride.

- Fox Delta Lima at the parking club, ready to roll.

- Fox Delta Lima, transponder 7000, QNH 1013, taxi to stop 34, through H, C and hold. Passing 2000 ft, contact Lyon approach 133.10.

I do not understand a word of the exchange between the pilot and the control tower. I detect that Fox Delta Lima is the beginning and the end of the registration of our aircraft F-DL. The plane starts to taxi from the parking lot along the yellow line, then stops. My hands are sweaty and my heart is pounding.

- Fox Delta Lima stopping point 34, ready to take off.

- Fox Delta Lima, line up on runway 34, cleared for takeoff.

- Fox Delta Lima, we line up and take off in 34.

We are in front of the track which lights up.

- Are you ready?

- Not really!

The plane accelerates. The runway goes by faster and faster. In a few moments, the nose of the plane rises. The wheels no longer touch the ground. We gain height and are now above the airport. I'm as tense as a popcorn on opening night. We climb into the sky as the sun sets. We make a 180-degree turn, Bron and the ring road disappear to make way for Fourvière, Part-Dieu, the Rhône, the Saône and everything that makes up Lyon. I feel like Anastasia in *Fifty Shades of Grey*. From his phone, he plugs in the music and, in my Bose headset which is connected, he plays "I believe I can fly, I believe I can touch the sky"[55]. The night falls, the lights of the city twinkle, it is magical.

I ask him about the instruments, I need to understand their meaning to be reassured, and listening to him talk to me about altimeters, artificial horizon and anemometers amazes me.

- You want to take the stick? The controls you have in front of you work perfectly. You want to fly?

- I am unable to take a selfie! My heart stops with every gust of wind. Let's go get a dry whiskey at the Selcius before I liquefy in midair!

The landing, although a bit tormented by the wind, was smooth. I get off the plane in a daze, I loved it and hated it. I am happy to have my feet on the ground, but the adrenaline that did not leave me along the flight makes me want to start again instantly. This is how I caught the aviation and love bug, despite the revelation of his first lie after a month of relationship: "Mathilde, I love

----

55. R. Kelly, *I believe I can fly*.

you, you are the woman of my life. For the first time, I feel alive, happy. At the beginning, it was just another adventure for me, so I lied to you. But I want us to make a real start. Think of my announcement as something unimportant. I'm married and have two children, but it's been years that with this woman we are just managers of a family, roommates and parents."

This love so strong that I too feel, this feeling of being one with the other and that nothing before existed, not even Nico, pushes me to close my eyes on her marital situation. I accept it, not caring about her. He puts me on such a pedestal that I forget she exists. I tell him about my past as an *escort*, my love affairs, my weaknesses, my strengths and nothing makes him waver. In his eyes, I am an exceptional being.

Three months later, we decided to create a business aviation company. I quit my job at the Confederation, gave up my weekend extra and embarked on this crazy project: "Don't worry, I'll be there to help you financially."

We want to make private aviation accessible to SMEs with the principle of shared ownership. I work night and day on the concept. I learn the regulations, the basics of aviation, the difference between private and commercial, the subtleties of this field. I am training myself to the point of knowing how to do the pre-flight inspection of a helicopter and to be perfectly credible when I interview a pilot. But my little cloud starts to turn into a storm. I discover by cross-referencing information that everything about this man is false and lies. Company shares that don't exist, villas that don't belong to him, aviation patents that he never took. He is contemptuous, oppressive, possessive, dissatisfied and extremely demanding. Nothing is ever good enough, sufficient or up to his standards: "Mathilde, in aviation you know nothing. I am the professional, you are just a whore trying to reinvent yourself.

Confiding in him, telling him my every secret, allowed him to use it against me. This incessant need to remind me of where I came from, as if he had pulled me up from the curb. As if one day I needed to be saved and I owed him everything. He constantly oscillates between talking about me in a positive way and talking about me in a negative way.

After working for almost a year to develop this project, I have no choice financially but to go back to work, as it doesn't help me. But I need time on the side to continue developing the business. I get up every morning at 4:30 am to go to the Novotel in Gerland and set up the breakfast buffet. I am recruited by Charlotte, the 26 year old manager, this little woman of barely 1.60m and 50kg is endowed with such intense energy that she seems to be on batteries. At dawn, her big green sparkling eyes breathe the joy of life and her dynamism brings you out of your morning sleepiness. Managing and organizing a buffet for four hundred customers, you have to be tightly knit, otherwise in a few dozen minutes the restaurant turns into a battlefield. Very quickly, we have a friendly crush. She was a lively person, always smiling and loved sunbathing in Miribel. That was already three things we had in common.

- Chacha, are we going to have a picnic on Sunday? I'm all alone, my boyfriend has a family dinner.

- I wonder, Mathilde, how you stand it.

- It's for the kids, I understand, and then he starts talking about separating from his wife.

- It starts to evoke! After one year!

Chacha and I come from the same social class, father in the trucking business, mother in the medical field, we know the difficulties of life, the importance of being united, and our upbringing in a modest environment has taught us the meaning of generosity and kindness of heart. Our friendship is new, but it is sincere. We can talk about any subject, have different opinions and expose our points of view. We respect each other's choices, even if they change, even fluctuate, from day to day. We just wish each other happiness. But I don't tell her about my past as an *escort*. I am today, in the eyes of all, a company director and the companion of a man. However, these two statuses are only a façade. Our company will never have a customer. It exhausts me and takes away the strength to sell it. In September 2016, he moves into my home and takes control of my entire life. I don't go to the gym anymore, because he's way too jealous to let me go and too lazy to go with me. I don't see my friends anymore, because if I'm not with him he harasses me with messages that I have to answer instantly. And he takes me to the four corners of France, we go to live in Paris, Valencia, and on the island of Principe, in the Gulf of Guinea. However, I do not exist. I am the suitcase he carries around, but which must remain in the hold, so that his wife does not see it. He plays with this love triangle that valorizes him. I have become everything I hate, a companion who obeys, bows her head and is humiliated in public: "Mathilde, when you have something interesting to say, you can talk."

I live the confinement, the psychological violence, the manipulation, the harassment, the destruction. For four years, he hit the same nail, me, until he drove it in so deeply that I no longer existed.

- Oh honey, you do realize that this guy is a psychopath. You can see it in his eyes. How long are you going to let him walk all over you?

- Elijah, I feel weak, I feel like without him I will be lost.

- But, you've already lost your way, my dear. You wanted to take off, but you crashed.

To be under someone's control seems inconceivable, but this kind of character, devoid of any empathy, masters perfectly the workings of psychology. I am the most wonderful woman and three hours later the most despicable person. I lose everything, he isolates me, my friends are not worthy, my family is made up of "little people" and staying at home waiting for him is better than working.

Almost four years after we met, on December 31, 2018, at 10:47 p.m., he is sitting next to me on the couch in our apartment. The bottle of wine he consented to open on this New Year's Eve, and which only he is allowed to serve so he can control my sips, is still almost full. A line from a movie he decided we should watch makes me think of Nico. I furtively Google his name in my phone, an obituary appears. I go to bed.

There are signs, interpretations, it doesn't matter, you have to catch the sparks and never let go. Life is too short, forgive me this new vulgarity, to let yourself be bored.

- It's over, I'm leaving you. Take your things and since you are still married, bring them back to your wife, in the closet you haven't emptied yet.

- If you leave me, we will die.

19. The crash of the century

I often see this image, I am in this car launched at very high speed on the highway, in which he made me enter by force. He pulls the handbrake, throwing our car through the safety barriers. But dying is better than being trapped for life. So I don't give up, I resist, I stand up to him even when he stages his suicide. I find him one evening, lying in his snot and drool, dying in the middle of a pool of drugs.

- I will never feel responsible for your death, and if you make your children orphans, I will never feel guilty.

That's all it took for him to get up, so he gives me one last death blow:

- It must be really hard, Mathilde, to come home and see that there is nothing left. I told you, without me you have nothing and you are nothing. But I'm not worried, you still have your ass.

From my panties to the Tupperware, from the bed to the candles, the plants, the curtains, the kitchen utensils, the appliances, the food, the medicine kit, in one afternoon, he took everything.

- Give me back the plants that I winter over and that go on my dad's grave.

- Don't bother me with your 10-bit stuff.

I imagined a thousand scenarios, tying him up in the forest of Miribel and leaving him naked all night long as a meal for the men who come to entertain themselves, throwing all his schemes to the authorities with proof, roasting him in the world of aeronautics so that he would never again fly even a drone, but my liberation from his hold was such that it was enough for me as a revenge.

20. I AM FREE

Now it's May 2019. Aurore is in my living room, drill in hand to fix my curtain rods and assemble my new furniture while I pop the champagne.

- I thought you were never going to leave him. How could you let yourself get involved in something like this? You, Mathilde? The strongest and most independent girl I know.

- Doctor Aurore, I'm not going to learn from you that I was the perfect target! Chacha sent me a Tinder screenshot, this crazy guy put me in his profile picture!

- He scares me Mathilde, are you sure you don't want to change apartments so he doesn't know where you live now?

- I love this apartment and it doesn't scare me anymore. You know very well that everything in his life is staged, everything is fake. Even when he tried to kill us on the highway, he did it under control. It's a very good news his Tinder, even if I don't wish it to any woman. He's looking for a new prey, he's done with me.

I arrived in Lyon ten years ago, and what did I like most during these ten years? When have I been happiest, most fulfilled, most free, most me? I am 35 years old, the age when a woman is normally a mother, married, divorced. I don't have any of that, but have I ever really wanted to? One of my mom's friends told me:

- Mathilde, my 42 year old daughter has just had her first child. It will soon be your turn.

- I don't think I want any.

- But yes, of course, all women want to be mothers.

- No, I'm not sure.

- But yes, when you meet someone good, you'll see.

- I guess you're right.

- Of course!

It's not wanting to, it's just going along for the ride. But where has it gotten me to be a woman in the norm? To not being respected, to being trampled on, to being put down and to being the object of a man or sometimes even a boss. So, it is certain that I was infatuated with a clinical case and that not all men behave like that. But from now on, there is no question of having a guy if he is not in perfect agreement with the person I am. Yes, I have been, am and will be a prostitute. I smoke, drink, not necessarily in moderation, talk loudly, alone, to my plants and in slang. I listen to Booba, Dalida, turn up the music in my car and moan at the wheel. I like pencil skirts, skaters, pumps, sneakers and jogging suits. I start a diet every Monday morning, and on Tuesday nights it ends. I sulk when I gain a pound and always negotiate to do as little as possible at the gym. I don't cook and I can't stand it when someone cleans for me, because I feel that things are better done my way. I go on vacation with my girlfriends and one-on-one with my buddies. And if all this is not acceptable, then I much prefer contractual relationships. The ones where I know the conditions beforehand, that don't commit to anything, that don't make me suffer, where I'm the "boss" who decides, defines the rules and disappears after an hour, taking her status of free woman and her independence with her. This is the life I like, not the one they try to impose on me. I have tried to fit into the mold, but I have to admit that the conventional framework has only destroyed everything that is good about me.

"I am Mathilda, bubbly, fun, relaxed, sporty, naughty and playful! For me, a successful date is a date where we both had fun. Send me a short introduction text message and let's call afterwards. I only travel. I like to meet gentlemen 35 years and older. I know that it is a bit difficult to reach me, I answer as I feel like it... Therefore, I take few calls. Kisses, Mathilda ".

I add to this little presentation text, on my new online ad, some pictures in sexy lingerie, always taking care to hide my face and camouflage my tattoos. I invest 200 euros in a Mobicarte, in a box of Skin condoms, in new panties, pairs of stockings and, on June 20, 2019, I am again referenced on the *listing* of girls available for paid encounters in Lyon.

My ad came out a day ago and I have over a hundred messages and calls. The market has not changed and I am at the top of the list on the site, which has almost two hundred ads for girls in the city.

"Hello Miss, I am Gilles, I am 62 years old. I am in Lyon. I am staying at the Mercure Lumière. I appreciate long foreplay, I am a greedy man. Can you tell me more about your expectations? I look forward to hearing from you."

"Hello, following a painful breakup, I would like to meet you. Mehdi, 30 years old, for a financially interesting duration."

"Hello, your ass is pretty bouncy for a French girl, don't you think?"

"Hi Mathilda, I prefer to tell you the truth, I'm 21 years old and I've never slept with a girl. I'm not particularly shy, but when I meet a girl I get stuck. I thought you could teach me a little, if you don't mind being my first experience."

"Are you doing the natural penetration? I want to spit in your pussy."

"Hello, I want a scenario. You walk down the street, I drive by, I stop at your height, you get in and you suck me off while I drive around Place Bellecour."

"Hi, we're two cool executives on the go. Are you available for a little good-natured shindig?"

"Hi, I don't know if this is you. I had the opportunity to meet a young woman who worked in a city hall and liked to play with vegetables. Is that you? If not, would you be interested?"

"Hello, my name is Louis, I am 35 years old, I live one hour from Lyon. I am in a wheelchair, but I am perfectly normal and very nice. I enclose a picture of me. Hoping to have a return. Kisses."

"Hello lovely Mathilda. My name is Will, I am 57 years old. I dare to hope that I am not too old for you. I am an epicurean, my hygiene is impeccable and my look is sporty. I would love to be able to meet you, what would be your terms? Yours truly."

I receive as before all types of requests from all types of men. From the craziest to the most classic. All I have to do now is to sort out and choose the profiles of men who correspond to me.

I only respond to messages with a presentation and to men over 35. Below that, they rarely have the money. And when they do, I know from experience that it's to get the most out of it, to fuck like a porn movie. This is not my niche, I prefer mature men who need seduction, to establish a bond, to increase the desire to find their pleasure. Men in their fifties are more concerned about their partner, they don't order an *escort* to do "dirty" to him. They invite a prostitute like one orders a pastry at Sébastien Bouillet's. We pay a lot of money for it, but we appreciate this moment, we long for it, we taste it, we don't devour it.

I don't answer to young virgin men either. I'm 35 and a 20 year old boy is not a man, but a child to me. The idea disgusts me, even if I've already fantasized about Killian Mbappé's muscular body, the sweat-soaked T-shirt that, as the game goes on, sticks to his torso allowing the curve of his abs to be drawn, his shapely buttocks in his shorts rising with each of his strides, run Killian, run! I doubt that he is the one who missions me to depucel him!

I don't respond to men with disabilities either, I wouldn't know how to do it and I'm not sure I'd be comfortable. It seems to me that only love could allow me to overcome this barrier. Here I am not looking for feelings, but for pleasure in all its forms, and my number one guideline is to do only what arouses my desire.

21. Who is my stranger?

For the first meeting, after five years of a conventional life, I selected Will. Our telephone exchange was pleasant, simple, and he seduced me with the sound of his dynamic voice, his laughing and relaxed tone. We have an appointment on Thursday, June 27, 2019, in the parking lot of the Leclerc shopping center in Francheville, at 4 pm.

I am wearing red lace lingerie, under a little sky blue summer dress, and a pair of lemon yellow heeled sandals. It is a scorching heat, I open my car. The village where we have an appointment is on the same side of the Lyonnais mountains as my apartment. We are almost neighbors. I cross the country roads, music blasting and hair blowing in the wind.

The man I am joining is 57 years old, this gap between us does not frighten me anymore. He just came out of a general assembly in the 6th district, according to his last message. He probably holds a position of responsibility, on the executive committee, which bodes well for an interesting exchange.

I feel like a young freshman going to a job interview after graduating from college, I'm a little feverish and nervous.

I haven't met a stranger in a long time, I'm afraid I won't be up to it and I'll feel uncomfortable. I'm not sure I'm still capable of leading a date, of keeping the discussion going and not leaving a gap that would cause a moment of embarrassment because, beyond sex, which is only the end, men expect me to be jovial, educated, natural, exciting. They don't want me to be bland and get naked and pretend to squeal before rushing off again.

I park in the mall parking lot, put the top down on my car and turn on the air conditioning while texting Will.

- I arrived, parked next to the pharmacy.

- OK, I'll take a scoot, I'll be right there.

A scooter, unusual at 57 years old! Who is going to show up? Would it be François Hollande my unknown ?!

A black two-wheeler type T max arrives a few minutes later. I get out of my vehicle to let him know that I am the one he has an appointment with. The heat is far too stifling to wait in a non-air-conditioned space and camouflage my vehicle before his arrival. He approaches me and takes off his helmet to greet me. He's not very tall, not much taller than me. He wears his hair back and his wavy, neatly combed mane is brown. He has a tanned complexion, almost Tropezian, and his bright teeth perfectly aligned give him a Hollywood look, an air of a movie star. He is dressed in faded blue jeans, patched and perforated, with a white polo shirt and a pair of Stan Smith. His modern look accentuates his age gap: "Hi, Mathilda, are you following me? We'll be back in two minutes. You will see on your left the Galtier parking, you park, you cross the road and you will find a small gate. You go in, I'll wait for you there, I'll put the scooter in the garage. See you soon."

Beyond his youthful, hip look, I have my doubts about his age. He doesn't look 57, but over 60. Either he looks older than his age and all his tricks are a bulwark against his early aging, or he lied to me. But I find him attractive, the kind of man we call "old handsome", attractive, dynamic and clean.

I still don't know who this atypical-looking character is. I can see in him a kind of familiarity with me, a way of being very spontaneous in his approach and an ease that lets me predict that he is a regular in public relations. I know the Galtier companies, the parking lot he points out to me, it is an institution in Lyon. There are about ten sales outlets, a few others in France and probably about a hundred employees.

I park my car in the parking lot of the company's headquarters. I see the offices, the warehouses, the delivery trucks, the cars with the effigy of the sign, the employees who are active or who smoke their cigarettes. On the other side of the road, I distinguish a big contemporary house with a flat roof and white facades. He is waiting for me at the entrance. I enter with wide eyes and see a patio where a swimming pool with asymmetrical curves is discreetly nestled. The surrounding slabs are made of light wood and a few scattered palm trees bring shade to the whole. The buildings and the vegetation that surround this peaceful space give me the impression of being in a riad in Marrakech. We walk along the glass roof to get to the kitchen and I am now in a "bouchon lyonnais". Everything is there, similar to the decoration of the Comptoir d'Abel. There is the stainless steel slicer, the sausages from Bobosse hanging from the ceiling with cords, the old iron plates on the walls representing places and specialities from Lyon, the big

21. Who is my stranger?

cast iron stove and the wooden table with an envelope with my name on it.

- Do you want to drink something cold?

- With great pleasure, it's hot as hell.

- Rosé, Perrier?

- A lemon Perrier would be great!

He is friendly and relaxed, my first impression has not disappeared. After the banalities about the weather conditions, we get to know each other better. I quickly regain my composure and my confidence, my anxiety of the departure has disappeared.

He does not hide and reveals to me that he is the boss of the Galtier establishments, that he also manages other brands and that he is very invested in the professional sports world. He is a business figure in Lyon and the number one in his field in France. Despite my interest in the economic fabric of Lyon, my years with the newspaper and the Confédération patronale, I did not know this man or his career, only his name and his empire. I follow with attention the news of start-ups and of our big companies, I admire the career paths and achievements of GL Events or Cardinal, among others. I am not a fan of song stars or actors, it is the *businessmen* who fascinate me. These business leaders are his friends, his associates.

We find we have a lot in common. He has tried ultralight flying and would like to learn to fly a helicopter. I have tried to launch a start-up in business aviation. He likes to hunt, I love the atmosphere of the Puces du Canal. He prefers motorcycle rides and hostels to aperitifs on the terrace of Sénéquier facing the yachts of Saint-Tropez. My best vacations are the ones when I linked Geneva to Lyon by bike and in a canvas tent with Aurore.

He confided to me that he was a regular in this type of meeting, he liked to maintain a relationship with the girls, to create an atmosphere that went beyond the tariffed side, but that never exceeded the limits. He does not talk to me about his personal life and I do not ask him any questions. He doesn't wear a wedding ring and I don't feel a female presence in the house. He asks me how long I've been doing this, I don't tell him he's the first, he really isn't. He is just putting my foot down after a long period of absence in this activity, more than five years.

I have been in his company for half an hour when he approaches me to give me a first kiss and proposes that we take a shower together. I do not feel, for the moment, any desire for him, only admiration.

I climb alone the suspended stairs that lead me to the second floor landing. I pass contemporary works of art that blend into this modern environment filled with home automation. I enter the room to drop my purse and take off my pumps. Will is still on the first floor. The night space measures 80 square meters. Two black suede armchairs are placed on a soft carpet in the same color. The floor is covered with a light parquet and the walls are half white, half *black matte*. The bed frame is inlaid in the materials and a few steps are needed to access it. Behind it are two skylights, one revealing the dressing room, the other the bathroom. My eyes scan the ornament of the room, a white stone Marianne as tall as me seems to stare at me and spy on me. However, it is not me that the statue is looking at, but this Ducati collector's model that sits in front of it. A red and white motor-cycle that looks old, but is shiny, like new. It bears the number 1 and above it hangs in a frame a picture of a man in a rider's outfit,

21. Who is my stranger?

helmet in hand and gold medal around his neck. The picture is signed with a black marker, I am not experienced enough to recognize the person or decipher the signature. I imagine that it must be the previous owner of the machine and that he won a race with it. That's pretty strange, who puts a real motorcycle in their room? Except for Johnny maybe! I furtively take a picture, this particularity amuses me, I want to keep a souvenir.

I hear Will go upstairs. I head for the bathroom. On a platform, the island bathtub on legs dresses the bottom of the room, which is just as big as the bedroom. At the entrance, there is an Italian shower, in front of it a white marble double sink, the same marble covers the floor and the walls. The lights of the spotlights change color and a *lounge* music sounds from a speaker representing a lion, in real size. No doubt, I am in a Lyonnais' home! I want the same at home! But I think my bathroom could not accommodate a speaker bigger than the representation of a cat!

I feel Will's breath on the back of my neck. I am startled, my back to him. He approaches slowly and, between kisses and caresses, I let him remove my small summer dress, unhook my bra and make slide my lace panties. He drags me delicately under the shower. Everything seems precious, the faucets are sparkling and the marble under my feet is cool and silky. We take care to lather our bodies respectively, his sex grows as my hand coated with soap makes back and forth on his member. He kisses my neck, rolls my nipples between his fingers, his gestures are soft, tender. He embraces me, runs his hands over my hips, my buttocks and delicately slides a finger inside my femininity. I feel him feverish. He gets out of the shower, wraps me in a soft towel and asks me to wait for him on the armchair. I sit there still wet.

The windows are open and the shutters ajar, I can hear the bustle of the business on the other side of the road.

He kneels on the ground in front of me and plunges his head between my thighs. I let myself go instantly. His gestures are both shy and intense. He awakens my senses and arouses my desire. He takes pleasure in licking me and I allow myself to enjoy it. I offer myself to him as one offers himself to a lover. His tongue, his fingers roam and penetrate my body. I close my eyes, pass my hands from his hair to my breasts. I squeeze her cheeks between my thighs and can't help but move back and forth with my pelvis to accentuate her tongue movements and increase my pleasure tenfold. I moan more and more, forgetting the open windows and the employees almost below. In a last wet and languorous impulse, I cum in his mouth thirsty of desire.

He takes my place on the chair and I take his on the carpet. His sex is stiff, thick, vigorous. My desire disappeared at the same time as my orgasm, I became masculine on that side! When I have cum, my partner doesn't interest me anymore. Then, I suck him greedily, I activate the mode mechanism to make him come quickly, but the man has cold blood and takes advantage of the extra that he offered himself. After several minutes of fellatio, he draws me into his bed, asks me for a condom and penetrates me like a missionary. I feel again desire and pleasure. He asks me to take me in doggy style and withdraws from my body to change position.

- Ah, you're on your period?

- No, why?

- There is a small drop of blood on the condom. I hate it, I can't, I'm sorry. Some men don't mind, I can't.

- No, I'm the one who is sorry, I'm not indisposed.

- Blow me, I'll come like this.

It's not a defensive reaction from my body, it's just poor schedule management and cycle tracking. I'm embarrassed, he's a little disgusted, but didn't end the performance.

I get out of the shower after making him come with my mouth. I don't accept oral sex, ever. There are certain practices that I keep for my personal partners. When I meet someone, I offer my breasts, my buttocks, my body or the condom.

- I'll give you half your money back.

I hope he refuses, but I am obliged to offer him a commercial gesture, it is part of my professional training.

- I really appreciate it, Mathilda, you don't have to offer me that.

- It's the least I can do, the order is not what you expected!

- No, I don't, but I really appreciate your offer. You're being honest, almost conscientious, if I can put it that way. But, I'd rather make you another offer. The next time we meet, you'll give me a discount, I won't take back the money I gave you.

- That's a great idea, Will, let's do that.

- Can you do me a favor? I have to pick up a car in a garage next door, can you drop me off there?

- Yes, no problem, with pleasure.

- I'm coming back from the United States on July 10, I'll call you then to see you again.

I felt comfortable with him right away, so I have no problem getting him into my car. I don't know the profiles of *serial killers*, but I doubt that he has already murdered one of his *escorts*. I've been paying attention to this kind of news in Lyon for a long time, the stories of prostitutes killed reported by the local press are common on the networks.

We get into my car, discuss mechanics and his upcoming trip, nothing could let us believe that our meeting is the result of a small ad. The trip lasts a few minutes, he gives me a friendly hug and promises to call me back, before getting out.

I put the car in first gear and drive a few hundred meters down a small country road. I reach into my purse and pull out my pack of Marlboro Gold. I light a cigarette and take a large puff of smoke before extracting the fifteen 20-euro bills from their envelope. The moment is enjoyable, like a few minutes before. These first 300 euros have a smell of freedom, I'm not an apprentice anymore, I've given myself a little raise. One of the advantages of this activity is that we are not bound by an agreement or minimum prices and we are the only ones to determine our rates. In Geneva, the hour is at least 700 euros, in Gerland you enjoy for 30 balls, and I determined that spending sixty minutes in my company was worth ten times more than that.

22. I TAKE THE SAME

- Hello, Mathilda? Hello, this is Paul. I'm taking the liberty of calling you, I saw your ad and I have a question. A few years ago, I saw a Mathilda I was a fan of, in Villeurbanne, is it you ?
- Paul, amazing! Yes, it's me, it's great to hear from you.
- So you're back, that's great, we're having lunch together?

***

- Hello, Mathilda, I'm Mickaël, are you the one who lived in Villeurbanne ?
- Mickaël, yes, indeed, it's crazy to hear you after so many years!
- I saw your ad, I thought it could only be you! Shall we arrange a meeting and you can tell me where you've been all this time?

***

- Hello, this is Olivier, from Vaise. Is that you, Mathilda?
- Yes, that's me!

- What a pleasure to hear you, you had disappeared without a word! I imagined you were married.

- And no, still not!

As incredible as it sounds, it's like Tinder! Eight years later, there are the same men on the *escort* sites. All three were among my regular clients back in 2012-2014, which is why my memory of them is intact. By the tone of their voice, I recognize them instantly. And it's like finding old friends or old booty calls. Time has passed, they are still there and I am back, but I am no longer that little 28 year old girl who is bored in her roommate's room and who decides to go out and have sex to occupy her evenings. I am 35 years old, and now I have faithful, sincere friends, with whom I don't invent a false life, all of whom are aware of my dating habits. Women and men from all walks of life, all ages and all social classes who, beyond being non-judgmental, have become true spokespersons capable of intervening in public by the strength of their convictions and who are offended by the contempt that society has for girls like me, TDS, sex workers: "I have a girlfriend who is an *escort,* and what is the problem? Tobacco kills, alcohol kills, and yet it's freely available. Since the invention of the condom, ass has never killed anyone, right?"

I also have men in my entourage that I met through this activity, in 2012, and of whom I have not drawn up a portrait, but who are still in my life without sex having its place. There is no ambiguity between us, I now know their wives and children.

I am no longer this kid in search of thrills, I am no longer even a young woman, but a woman. I am more often in the mood to celebrate than to be depressed, I am benevolent, attentive, I give without expecting to receive. I have an atypical personality, now it's not just "they say", I've become aware of it. I know that I have a frankness that can be unpleasant, I am one of those people that we love or hate. I am not afraid of what I think and say. I am not always very diplomatic, but I have been working on it for many years. I analyze quickly, get to the point and rarely bother with the embroidery necessary to get a message across smoothly, I understand that this can be irritating. People sometimes say that I am arrogant, haughty, different. I often express what others hardly dare to think, it is disturbing and my humor is close to Baffie's, piquant. So, without second degree, it can be hurtful. But, I try to become the best version of myself. I listen, I learn, I try not to stick to my guns and I try to adapt, even though I've never been able to say "Yes, yes" and put my head down. I am willing to temper, but I will never be resigned. If I had to choose only one quote, I would choose the one of Abbé Pierre: "The greatest failure is not having the courage to dare".

Since you already have the "no", it doesn't cost anything to try to get the "yes". Believing in yourself is not easy, it's a daily struggle, but 100% of the winners have played. So let's play, otherwise nothing will happen.

When I had my aviation company, I stopped politicians in the street, beat the code to get meetings with the biggest entrepreneurs in the area, and it worked. Don't put any barriers or limits on yourself, even if it doesn't work this time. I often say that I have nothing to lose today, but a lot to gain tomorrow.

By resuming *escorting* after my breakup, I probably chose the easiest and most obvious way, but it's the only thing I want, a bit of *dolce vita*. My vision of things has evolved, I know the environment. I'm not interested in abundance, nor in owning things. Only the freedom that this activity brings me is important to me. The freedom of time, financial, sexual, the possibility of living each day as I want, without commitment, but having the possibility of making exciting meetings.

I choose when, where, with whom and how much.

Paul is now in his early fifties, is the father of four children and owns a company that sells agricultural machinery. A few days after his call, we have lunch together in a small Italian restaurant down the street from my house. He has aged, and so have I, but he is no less handsome. We had never had lunch together before, but a return after five years of absence deserves an update. I tell him my life story, as I tell everyone I haven't seen in years. I know he was a little bit in love with me back then and I have a feeling he still is. He writes to tell me he misses me, hugs me when I get to his house, hugs me and makes love to me. Sometimes he fucks me and tells me I'm good, but he's always full of tenderness. I like him and I satisfy a sexual desire. Our relationship has become routine, like an old couple. I always see him at noon, arrive when the cleaning lady leaves and leave before his wife arrives. But when I think about it, he just likes to make love to me. In less than five minutes we are naked and twenty minutes later I am gone. We exchanged five sentences:

- I missed you, my darling. You look so good!

- Thank you. How are you doing at work right now?

- Yes, I'm fine.

***

- You're still as good as ever. Will you stop by next week?

- Yes, if you want. We write to each other, we keep in touch.

Let's just say he loves me in his own way. And so do I.

I also see Mickaël again. I have always liked this man, tall, handsome, in his forties. I found him in a bachelor apartment in Villeurbanne, and he welcomed me with a big smile, as usual. He is very attentive, notices if I have cut my hair, if I have a new necklace or if I have lost weight. His thing is cunnis and he is on the podium in the realization of this art, so I always let myself go during our little meetings.

Olivier, Bernard Henri Lidl, has not changed his practices, but his lifestyle does not allow him to *book* me as regularly. He is however *registered* in my VIP *listing* and receives my best wishes for the New Year, like all those I appreciate.

A few weeks after having resumed this way of meeting people, I accepted an appointment at the Ibis budget, Grande rue de St Clair in Caluire, at 3 p.m., under the pretext that the young man seemed nice on the phone. His name is Bastien, he is 38 years old, and he is travelling to Lyon for the day. I arrive at the entrance of the hotel, he waits for me outside: "The room is not yet available, I'm sorry, the receptionist is working as fast as possible."

We wait in the shade, next to the building. He tells me a little about his life, is nice, but strange. He enters again in the hotel then leaves it. The room is not ready, we still have to wait. After twenty minutes, I'm still on the sidewalk thinking: "What do I do, do I go, do I stay?" I don't go into the lobby, I don't want the staff to be able to associate me with them. I don't know what he's doing, what he's talking about, I have doubts about his story. He doesn't have the profile of a policeman, the subject would have been launched and I don't know if it is really done the censuses of prostitutes. He does not have the behavior of a pimp who would be there to recruit me, the room would have already been rented and I would be sequestered there. He comes back a third time, annoyed: "She's making me mad, we'll find another solution. Do you mind if we do this in my car? Just, you suck me off, but I'll give you the money like we said."

Between my preparation, the drive and the wait on the sidewalk, I just spent two hours of my time with him. We are far from luxurious appointments. An old wrecked station wagon in a parking lot below the hotel. I did it. Then I *blacklisted* it in my directory.

A blow job in a car, we have all done it to our lover, but this is not how I see my art of living. Prostitution, yes, but our body must be a luxury product for those who wish to afford this pleasure. A product, but not an object. And I am the only one who can make my conception, my reality. The race for money cannot be a *leitmotiv* in this field, without the risk of getting lost. Abundance leads to bad encounters, a too lax selection leads to degrading situations, a low rate sends you directly into the lion's den. When you wear overalls, you don't pay attention, when you wear your best white shirt, you don't venture to eat spaghetti. When you have something precious, you take care of it.

I allow myself this gap, but I am now too clear-sighted to accept a second one. I start again this activity to allow me to be free, independent, but I want luxury, glitter, champagne and orgasms. Even if it means earning less, even if it means meeting few people.

- Mathilde, since you're back to this way of life, why don't you make a lot of money?

- Because to make a lot of money, you have to accept everything, Aurore. And I don't want to meet several men a day or do things I don't like.

Most of the time, I can detect the personality behind the screen and I am rarely unpleasantly surprised. I trust my instinct and the questions I ask. Nevertheless, I am not immune to certain lies or tricks, as with Gerard, 47 years old, fireman, on a training course in Lyon. He *booked* me for two hours in a small hotel in Perrache. This district was the hub of street prostitution a few years ago in Lyon. The new constructions and the rehabilitation of the Confluence area made my colleagues move to the other side of the bridge, in Gerland. There are still a few girls walking along the Perrache quay, but they are discreet. This hotel on the edge of the A7 freeway has seen a large number of "clandestine sex workers" come and go. It's a little cold and entry-level, but I tell myself that the barracks are certainly not going to offer a four-star hotel to their firefighter at taxpayer's expense. I cling to the fantasy of the firefighter, it's sexy, exciting, which will compensate for the lack of prestige of the place. We have an appointment at 2 pm.

He opens the bedroom door, I break down.

- Hello, Gérard, thank you for seeing me.

- Hello, Mathilda, but my name is Denis.

- Denis, sorry, I was convinced that your name was Gerard. I wrote it down wrong, I'm really sorry.

Everything gets mixed up in my head. I was convinced that I was coming to meet Gérard, a fireman, but I am facing Denis, small, bigger than me, twice as big as me and with one tooth less on the front. I am destabilized. I am angry at myself for not having paid attention before my arrival, the appointment was made a week before. At what point did I reverse the profiles? What did I mix up? Having already got my name wrong, I don't say, "But aren't you supposed to be a handsome, athletic fire-fighter? Because I'd made a movie of you with your muscles bulging out from under your uniform, carrying me at arm's length and throwing myself on the bed to put out the fire that's burning my body."

I can't get away. When I arrive, he offers me a bag of nougats from Pierre Bonnieu, the artisan from Montélimar. He is adorable and even the little fat ones have the right to enjoy life.

- And what are you doing in Lyon?

- I am in training, I am a craftsman-heating engineer. I come to validate a specificity to have an accreditation and to be able to make heat pumps.

But to occupy two hours, sometimes it is very long. When the *feeling* is not there or when an element comes to disturb the initial scenario, it is necessary to adapt and try not to let anything show. Not because this man is paying me and I have to be devoted to him for the given time, no, simply because he is a human being and he is nice to me. I can't make him feel that his physical appearance is a hindrance in the good progress of our meeting, it would be insulting.

I am curious by nature, so I am always resourceful when it comes to leading a discussion to fill the time. He traveled a lot, I was interested in each country, the customs, the gastronomy, the temperature of the lagoons and the color of the sky at sunset. I tried to transport myself to the paradisiacal beaches of which he praised the beauty.

When he started to lick me and said: "You like that, huh? Huh, you're a little slut? Huh, you're my bitch? Tell me you're a slut."

Getting only an "umm, yes" from me, he dispatched the act, left the closed bottle of champagne on the windowsill and said, "Me, I'm going for a walk."

I have nothing against the raw words, I even find it rather exciting, but on the condition of being excited! I left after fifty minutes, with my two hours booty and my bag of nougats that I offered to my tobacconist, for the anecdote.

I looked at our exchanges in my phone and I was not mistaken, he had introduced himself as a fireman. I don't know what made him invent a profession. Had he been turned down before with honesty? Was it my ad in which I mentioned my desires that compelled him to hand me a carrot? Or had he been a volunteer firefighter in his youth and, like people who post a fifteen-year-old profile picture on the networks, he was stuck in the past and in his fantasy of himself?

Surprised, I felt in front of him like this miss to whom Jean-Pierre Foucault said: "Miss France is Miss Rhone-Alpes. Oh no, sorry, Miss France is Miss Burgundy."

If Jean-Pierre hadn't told you that you had won, you would have accepted second place better. If I hadn't imagined a handsome firefighter, I wouldn't have felt cheated and would have overlooked his unattractive physique.

- Are you done yet? The fireman couldn't light the fire hose?

- Chacha, don't tell me about it!

- You got caught in your own trap, the Ibis in Perrache, frankly Mathilde, I thought you were more professional than that, you disappoint me!

22. I take the same

- But he must have been a fireman!

- Firemen put out fires, Mathilde, they don't start them! Come by the house, you're lucky, I'm ready.

After years of hiding my past as an *escort* from the woman who was my boss three years ago when I was doing extras at the Novotel Gerland, and who has now become one of my best friends, I couldn't help but bring my expertise to her when one day she told me: "I think my guy is banging hookers.

My confidences on the subject did not really reassure her about her relationship, but I think I at least gave her a broader view of prostitutes.

- Mathilde, I'm not going to tell you that you are right and that we should all do this, but your insight and empathy make you a healthy person. You always have a kind word and a caring attention, even when telling me your stories with your clients. You're a bit of a weirdo, it's true, but I don't have to try very hard to understand your choices. I'm not sure I can do that, although when I think about it, not all the guys that have banged me have been into me. I often gave myself away in the hopes of receiving something, affection, interest or even a pint of beer!

- For a pint of beer, I don't even give the time of day!

- Liar! For a smile, you'll strike up a conversation with anyone!

23. I WANT AN *ESCORT BOY*!

It's late summer 2019. I stopped at the wine shop to pick up some red wine, a Saint-Joseph from Chapoutier, a charcuterie board from Sibilia, a cheese board from Mons for an aperitif dinner with Aurore and Chacha. A Deezer *playlist is* running and Dadju sings:

"Me, fall in love with this kind of girl, I would never have believed it, I add a thousand euros, so that you become the love of my life, Another thousand euros, so that the other men you forget them"[6].

- Are we doing anything on Friday?

- I can't, I have an appointment at the Intercontinental with Sebastien.

- Sebastien?

- A customer I've already seen, a few weeks ago at the Sofitel Bellecour. Handsome according to my memories, even if I don't really remember what he looks like! But, I remember having a nice time and my comment about him is positive, so the evening should be nice.

---

6. Dadju, *Escort.*

- Your comment? Do you keep a file with comments about your clients?

- Yes, so I remember who is who! What I've told them, what they do for a living, what they like in bed, how old their kids are, where they went on their last vacation and what outfit I wore on our date, so I don't wear the same one twice. And when I see them again, I know what to expect. Plus, they're always happy that I remember them and their special features!

- That's a good point! Do you read us what you wrote?

- Monday, July 8, 2019, 8pm, Sofitel. Sebastien, 37 years old, preppy young man's face, glass of rosé at the hotel bar, nice chat, manages fifty employees at Canon, cool sex, nice cock, small fellatio, did a lot of interruptions to not cum, took me doggy style, I climbed on him for a minute before he cum. That's it, end of commentary!

The girls explode with laughter.

- But you are completely crazy, Mathilde! You killed me with laughter! Do you have another one?" asks Chacha.

- Random: August 2, 2019, Hotel Kyriad, Saint-Genis-Laval, 1pm. Jérémy, in fact his name is Abdel, had given me a false first name, rebeu, company manager in digital solutions, loves to be shot, kiffed me like crazy, hyper nice, BL MSG. Oh yes, I remember him.

- What does BL MSG mean?

- Blacklisted see messages! I remember very well why, finally, after our rather pleasant date, I blocked him. He tried to put some pressure on me by sending me messages that we should have a private, non-priced relationship.

- Seriously, he had a crush!

- He's got a kick in the ass instead! He just doesn't want to pay anymore. And under the pretext that I was nice, he tries. There was no intellectual or sexual connection between us. There's Tinder for free sex, and I don't have a profile on Tinder!

I talk freely with all my friends about my dating style, hiding it would mean that it is shameful and that is not how I live it or perceive it. It may be unconventional, it may even be rather unconventional, but I accept it. I tell them my stories, as they tell me theirs. So, there is more sex in mine, but isn't that the ingredient we add to every sauce? This spice that we add to spice up any dish lacking in flavor? This little "spice" that enlivens our evenings, our conversations, our thoughts?

In between appointments, I'm spending the summer of 2019 partying, going on weekends with my girlfriends.

I met up with a long-time friend from Marseille and we chose Bordeaux as our base. We rent a 4 star hotel to celebrate her upcoming wedding.

- Mathilde, I'm getting married and I want to have a party. Only with you can I do that, I want to order an *escort boy*!

- So, it's not a legend, women have really turned into guys!

- I want to try it once in my life! I don't see why only men should be able to have this little pleasure!

- But, I totally agree with you. I'm going to call the hotel concierge, I'm sure they'll be able to get this for us!

- Hello, good morning. I am in suite 720, I would like to know if you have any *escort* phone numbers to give me?

- Yes, ma'am, absolutely, we have that. What profile would you like?

- Two men in their thirties and older.

23. I want an escort boy!

- I'm sorry, ma'am, I only have female *escorts.*

- I find this unacceptable. You should show a little more parity in the selection of your services, dear sir, and think about your female clientele. Satisfying your rich male clientele is no longer enough!

- I'll pass on your suggestions, ma'am, but I'm not sure if there are men who offer this type of service.

- Don't be fooled, the *escorting* websites are full of offers.

- I take note and inform you, madam, that I leave my service at midnight.

- Am I to understand that you wish to make up for your failure?

- Absolutely, ma'am.

The dedication of luxury hotel staff has no limits, and this young man saw in this request the chance of a lifetime: two chicks, drunk, euphoric and ready to order two *escort* boys. He offered himself gracefully to my friend and I left the room, I had no maidenhood to bury!

That summer, I took the first trace of cocaine in my life, because I had to try it, and "No, but don't worry, it doesn't do anything". But if the drug has no effect, why take it? The whole club l'Imprévu still remembers it! I'm already a little *fast in* normal times, but now I'm unleashed. I have an overflow of love, the least stranger I meet becomes my best friend and if I see a friend, my feelings are multiplied tenfold. Comparable to MDMA, they say. I've never tried it, but I hear that having sex on MD is magical, incredible.

It is in this slightly euphoric state, mixed with the desire for novelty and change, that I accept the festive offer of two 40-year-olds passing through Lyon. "On the other hand, boys, I don't do double penetration, nor anal. I want to come and have fun with you for an evening, to party, to laugh, but I don't propose anything with the word double!"

Anal lovers must think I'm missing something. I hear that sodomy and double penetration are incomparably pleasurable. As for having two men for yourself, the idea is exciting, isn't it?

"Mathilde, tell us some crazy stories, some funny stuff." I am often asked this, I intrigue, I arouse curiosity and I must have anecdotes. Preferably, a story that is a little dirty, creepy or very dirty. Yes, especially very dirty!

I set off to meet these two athletic and educated apollos, two lawyers in suits and ties and carefully polished shoes, in a pretty villa with a swimming pool, rented by Airbnb in the Lyon countryside. An absolute discretion, an evening where fantasy can give way to reality. Two men to satisfy me, to fulfill me. Isn't it one of the most common fantasies for women? To delight in one, when the other delights in himself. To feel the virility and the pleasure of the first one in the softness of our mouth when the second one satisfies our excitation by torrid back and forth between our thighs. One in the mouth, one in the pussy, some will add: "and one in the ass". Ladies, let's not be ashamed. Yes, it's exciting to let ourselves be guided, to give in to our desires, to be the center of interest, the being to be filled, to be ecstatic. A man openly exposes his desires, his fantasy of two women, two goddesses who give him a two-mouth fellatio and whose rumps are held out to him as an offering. I am sure that many of us have heard our companion mention it, "in jest". How many of us have dared to say: "I'd like to fuck another guy with you. I'd like you both to eat my pussy at the same time. Watching you fondle each other. And that I can switch from one cock to another as I feel like it." Oops! Gross!

But this experiment that made my panties wet on the way to the appointment was a fiasco. Apollo and Apollo bis did not survive their little party. "Apollo, do you read me? I think the rocket doesn't want to take off!"

I don't know if our bodies react differently or if it's the quality of the product that provides opposite effects, but for some people cocaine multiplies endurance, for others it takes the wind out of their sails.

I promised pigs, but I was left with fantasies. To party properly is not given to everyone! We drank, danced, snorted. Fucked, on the other hand, not really. When one can't get it up, the other won't give it up! This duo of Masters pleaded for solidarity, so we did a karaoke! If they had said to me, "Tonight, honey, you're going to sing into our microphones!", I would have thought it was a comical metaphor, not reality.

So, rather than trying new disappointing sexual experiences (!!), I think about a new professional project in parallel with my appointments.

24. You are not my bitch

In September 2019, I decided to launch a YouTube channel: "How to combine abs and appetizers", salesman and tempting, right?

- Mathilde, my daughter, what are you getting into now? Couldn't you have a normal job like everyone else?

- The Web is the future, Mom.

- All this is beyond me, social networks, YouTube, it's not a job.

In exchange for the rewriting of the texts of his website and small administrative works, a friend who runs a video studio lends me the services of his cameraman and his editor. A friend in communication takes care of the layout of my commercial brochure, in exchange for a good restaurant. I approach sports shops to get discounts on equipment, I contact climbing gyms, boxing gyms and high level athletes to test their discipline, and I approach restaurant owners to cook with them. I open an Instagram account, buy "how to become an influencer" trainings. I try to understand the codes of this environment and this new profession. I post *stories* daily, shoot more professional videos with partners who accept it. I spend hours, days, nights to increase my number of *followers*. I organize contests to win trial sessions or tickets for sporting events.

"Will, can you give me tickets to the event you are sponsoring, I'd like to run a contest on my Instagram page?" As promised, upon his return from the US, we met again. Will has become my friend, my mentor. He invites me to parties he hosts, introduces me to his associates, saves me a seat in the VIP boxes at events he sponsors. He calls me his *coach*. He doesn't play sports, everyone knows that, but everyone pretends to believe our little charade. I find it amusing. He checks on me when I'm sick, has lunch with me to talk business, fixes my car when it has problems. I have immense respect and admiration for this man. His career is incredible and his simplicity exemplary. I love it when he makes love to me, and this has been the case since the first time, and I love spending time with him. He must certainly appreciate the young woman I am, beyond the sexual aspect of our relationship. He tells me that the most important thing in life is to be happy and that the rest is of little importance, I agree with this philosophy. I don't know if he sees other *escorts* or if I am his only mistress, but if one day we are no longer intimate, he will always be part of my entourage. I matter to him and I have a special place. He includes me in his personal life, he invited me to his birthday lunch with his closest friends. There were about ten of us at the table, I was the only woman.

- Do you think, Will, that the people you introduce me to think I'm your bitch?

- But, first, you're not my bitch.

I don't know what I am to him, but he is the very example of why I like to do this type of meeting. Because yes, beyond the sexual aspect, a client and a prostitute can form a real bond. I now know his friends and have introduced him to some of mine.

In parallel to the creation of my YouTube channel, I only answer requests from my regular clients and businessmen passing through luxury hotels. I schedule very few appointments, I have a rotation that is sufficient for my essential needs. I have my head in my project, like every time I undertake something, I have no room for superfluous. Months go by, I postpone the launch of the channel, I don't like the editing of the videos. I install a software on my computer, try to train myself via tutorials, not so easy with general public equipment and an aversion for computers. The end of the year is approaching, we are already in December 2019.

A few days before Christmas Eve, as usual, we have dinner with Tom, my friend from the restaurant. It is our meal of end of the year. In the afternoon, he calls me: "I planned a small present for you, my Mathilde."

Damn, I have nothing! I go to the press house to buy a pack of scratch cards, I find that it always puts a nice atmosphere to imagine becoming a millionaire in a moment.

- Math', what do we do if we win the jackpot?

- First, I make all the people I love rich. And then I become a *business angel* and invest in start-ups.

- I'll make you a child!

Often, he tells me this: "You are the woman of my life, but you don't know it yet!" Face to face at the aperitif, after having won 5 euros and seen our dreams fly away, he hands me a package wrapped in newspaper. I remove the wrapping and discover a square box from Louis Vuitton, the packaging for the belts tied with a red fabric. I open the little drawer and Tom's perfume fills my nostrils instantly. A white sheet of paper is folded in four, on which is written in pencil:

" Mathilde,

Just this little message to tell you that I love you... It's always good to hear it. Our last years have not been easy for both of us, but it's supposed to make us stronger... I hope to take off soon for a new project... I'm not the best at messages, you know me (lol). You are and will remain MY MATHILDE, my buddy, my confidant, the prettiest, the craziest, maybe one day in my bed (lol). I love you."

Signed with his first and last name.

I could have cried, because receiving a letter is the most touching gift. It is not about material things, but about emotions and feelings, the most precious thing in life.

"Words fly, writings remain"[7] .

2020 is here. I have a thousand *followers* on Instagram, a far cry from the fifty thousand needed to start considering lucrative partnerships. I'm starting to run out of steam and the Covid wind is coming. Hotels are slowly emptying. My requests for meetings are cancelled. The sentence falls: *stay at home.*

- I told you, Mathilde, that it was serious. You didn't want to take things seriously, as always.

- Yes, indeed, my little mother, you are probably right. But who could have believed all this? Who would have imagined that one day we would be forced to stay locked up at home? Fortunately, Chacha and I spent a crazy weekend partying in Lyon!

---

7. From the Latin *"verba volant, scripta manent".*

- The party's over, Mathilde. Promise me to stay at home, not to see anyone, not to take any risks.

Not taking any chances may be too late for me. During the first two weeks of March, I saw a man returning from Gabon and another from China. I am surely sick, I may have contaminated my girlfriends. Not seeing anyone, my life is made of meetings, I started *escorting* again six months ago. Not going out, cutting myself off from the world, everything that is part of my daily life is collapsing like a house of cards. Like many of us, my life is completely turned upside down. I worry about my friend Aurore, a resuscitator now in the hospitals of Lyon: "For the moment, it's okay, we lack equipment, but for the moment we manage."

I am also worried about my mother who is 68 years old and has to cut herself off from the world, from her grandchildren. I worry about my sisters, the ones who often have everything taken away from them and don't have much. Will worries about me: "Hey Chica, how are you? Stay home, I'll check on you as soon as I can, it's just a bad time."

A bad moment to spend? I stay in a loop in front of CNews one day, two days, three days, I am like a lion in a cage.

25. THE INVISIBLES

April 2020, it's been almost a month since France is confined and I haven't been able to meet anyone. The current climate is too tense and the risks are very high. We do not have enough information on this new disease and my activity is among those most directly exposed, but as it is impossible for me to work with a mask and to respect social distancing, I have put myself in isolation, waiting to learn more.

I am one of the independent workers without status, the unrecognized shadow workers. So, during the pandemic, we had no help, no support and no thought from the State. And the media on their side ignored our case. Prostitution does not exist in France, and prostitutes even less. There are those who work on the side of the road in a van. The ones we meet in the evening while walking our dog and who wander along the quays or the streets, which have become, by their presence, ill-famed. Those on the outskirts of the countryside who give the impression of living in their van and who never seem to leave their place. The ones we don't see, the Internet girls. Whatever, they are a real scourge for the cities and their inhabitants. So to no longer see these young women draining a disgusting audience is a relief, almost a victory for some. There is no shortage of this so-called promiscuous workforce and no one is interested. How did we manage to live and pay our bills during this first confinement? No one is concerned. Our distress is silent, therefore unencumbered. We are not able to express ourselves. Our shaky status, the shameful pressure of society, the feeling of being pests who have no rights but who should still fulfill certain duties, prevent us from exposing ourselves publicly. So, no matter what happens to us in the eyes of others, we just didn't have to go down that road.

I had some savings left over, but not enough to put the risks of COVID-19 ahead of my main source of income. And even though I have learned to live alone, I am not a loner by nature. I need to meet people to feel alive.

2020 was supposed to be the year of glory. The year 20/20. We had never thought about the subtraction 20-20 = 0.

So what happens now? I usually get up early, at 6:15am, because even though I don't have office hours, rules to follow, I set a time frame for myself, no way am I going to hang out in bed until 10am. When the sun comes up, I want to live with it and go to CrossFit for the 7am session. But even the sport that keeps us fit is taken away from us. From now on, I try to sleep until 8 am so that the day is not too long. I plug in the news, depressed in front of Pascal Praud's ads. I cut the ringing of my professional phone, do not recharge it and it turns off by itself.

I'm losing the taste for performance and don't post anything on social networks anymore. I keep my sports habits, I have some equipment at home, I'm lucky to have space. So I work out in my living room every day. At 9 am I work out and at 11 am

I roll my first joint. I do this for a whole month. Normally, I'm a very casual user. However, I don't touch a single drop of alcohol, not sure if that deserves a good point. I don't see anyone, don't *FaceTime*, don't even answer my girlfriends' calls. I'm sad, I don't want to do video, I want to see people in real life, not through a screen. I miss my life and my escapades too.

I'm lying if I say I was stronger than myself during that first confinement. I don't read a single line of a book, don't sort through any of my papers, don't empty my closet. Some days I even feel like dying. Fortunately, I don't do that either. Weeks go by, sure that I am not contaminated or contagious, I see my girlfriends again, a brunch here and there under the cover of a "compelling family reason" certificate. Living alone yes, living isolated no.

I'm creating a Tinder account, but making virtual acquaintances almost blindly to meet guys who just want to fuck me... it's a bit too much like *escorting*, without the extra touch that goes with it. Besides, Elijah told me that there are more and more *escorts* on Tinder. The pictures are explicit and there is a little smiley face € in the description.

In May 2020, still during confinement, I go on a mountain bike ride with a friend I met during my CrossFit sessions. We don't know each other very well, but we live in the same countryside. And during this period of confinement, it is almost vital to find allies close to home. Elise is a 40-year-old divorced woman and mother of two. Although we have discussions on all sides, I have never discussed my double life with her. It's not a topic I bring up in a budding friendship. I know from experience that trust is earned. We had been riding our bikes for three hours through forests, vineyards and fields when, at the end of a bend leading to a suburban area, I came face to face with Coco, a stroller at arm's length. We stared at each other, but didn't exchange a word. Eight years later, our bitterness has not disappeared.

I must admit that I mumbled something unpleasant to him.

- You know her, you seemed to be staring at each other?

- An old acquaintance, Elise, nothing more.

26. Negative PCR test

I turned on my work cell phone again on May 10, 2020, the day before the deconfinement. Only about ten people had tried to reach me. On the 11th, my phone goes crazy. You want to live too, apparently. Within a few hours, I was inundated with calls and requests for appointments. I have a feeling that all men need to let go after this period of confinement. Single men have overconsumed porn movies, dating sites and loneliness, those in a relationship have *overdosed* on their partner. I feel the human distress, the unconditional desire to live and the need for carefree living of everyone. The disease is far away and no longer exists, at least for the space of an appointment.

"Hello, Mathilda, finally we are free! Can you come to my place in Lyon Croix-Rousse, for an evening? I am negative, test done today. Pascal, 48 years old, respectful, normal physique."

This is one of the new things after Covid. I have never received a check-up from the men before, none of them have ever written to me or said, "I don't have an STD". Now I receive their PCR results by MMS. But I am not worried about the risk of the disease anymore, I am not normally prone to the severe form. It's getting back into a seduction mode after two months of isolation that is difficult, like when we stop sports, putting on sneakers and going for a run becomes the test of a lifetime. I didn't stop physical activity during the first confinement, but like most of us, I hung out jogging in my apartment, eating chips and cake in front of Netflix series. I got fat, depressed and let nature take over my body. I don't have hair on my legs, but almost hair, my hands don't know what it's like to be manicured, I can't remember my face with makeup on it and my last blow-dry was three weeks ago. I need to brush myself off, dust myself off, get back to the social state, put on my seductress costume to answer the calls again. And just like a telemarketer who recites her script that she knows by heart, my speech on the phone is always the same, and the automatisms come back quickly. I know my lines inside out, I have a perfect command of the hidden interview that I give to the men, it is the same for everyone. Everything is smooth and square, I lead the conversation. I establish a friendly but courteous contact from the very first seconds. I tease my interlocutor, about soccer if he comes from Paris or about the weather if he comes from Lille. I probe his reactions, I need to guess the man behind the phone who is able to tell me what he wants. So I judge him by relying on the charter that I have developed and that I have been working on for years.

Does he speak normally or does he speak softly? Is he jovial, pleasant, natural? Is he embarrassed when he expresses a desire or a fantasy? Does he get offended when I ask him personal questions, about his field of activity, for example? Is he inclined to reveal himself to reassure me? Or does he remain distant, defensive and eager to keep any form of anonymity?

- Your questions are far too intrusive, Miss. I am not contacting you to seduce you.

- In that case, we won't go any further with the exchange, sir. You are not the kind of man I like to meet.

To hear him express himself allows me to categorize him, the voice reveals certain aspects of the personality. I like to hear the smile, the sympathy and the honesty in the tone of the vocal cords. Our conversation must be fluid, like an Orange teleconsultant talking to a potential subscriber. Everything must seem perfectly natural and spontaneous so that my interlocutor doesn't dehumanize himself and doesn't forget that, even if our relationship is priced, I am a woman, not an object.

I don't go on a date thinking that I'm going to have sex with a man I don't know, I just think that I'm going to discover a new person. A person that I will have selected carefully. Maybe she will be interesting, the hotel pleasant, the champagne fresh and I will let myself go naturally and take pleasure in addition to the money.

- Hello, Mathilda, I am following up on your ad that caught my attention. My name is Stéphane, I am 49 years old, I am 1m80 tall and weigh 78 kg, I have blue eyes and brown hair. I am an airport manager and my look is quite sporty. I have an impeccable hygiene. Can you tell me more about your conditions and your services? I look forward to hearing from you. Sincerely your Steph.

- Hello Stéphane, thank you for your message and your charming presentation. I suggest that we call each other to discuss in person. When would you be available? Love Mathilda.

I decided to respond to his message, as he fit my selection criteria and seemed to be able to offer me a pleasant evening for

26. Negative PCR test

this confinement outing. He is courteous and has made an effort to write without spelling mistakes, and in correct sentences. And even though his message is a cut and paste one that he sends to many of my sisters, he took care to personalize his introduction, although it was very formal. He gave me a rather enticing description of himself and highlighted his physical assets to seduce me. He talked about his social status to reassure me, the manager's hat can be seen as a guarantee of security. He goes into detail about his sector of activity, because it reinforces his seriousness, and he scores even more points with me. Safety, seriousness, but above all aviation, I know this environment well and never tire of evenings talking with pilots or other actors of the aeronautics.

- Can I call you now?

- Yes.

***

- Hello Mathilda, this is Stéphane. I really liked your ad and I would like to know how to get the chance to meet you.

- Hello Stéphane, thank you very much. I appreciate being addressed in the same way, it's respectful and very important to me. I don't like to be called by my first name and I note your good education. But if you agree, do you think we can be on first-name terms now? It will be more pleasant and friendly to exchange.

- Yes, of course, with pleasure.

- First of all, Stéphane, I like to know who I'm dealing with. You gave me a little description in your message and I thank you for that, but you didn't tell me if you are from Lyon or just passing through?

- I am from Lyon, from Caluire. I am 49 years old, dynamic, sporty, epicurean and I like to enjoy life! I can even add, without any pretension, that people say I am handsome.

- Dynamic, sporty, epicurean and handsome! It is an explosive cocktail of qualities! Be careful not to disappoint me! Did you see that I only move, I do not receive, is it something that can suit you?

- Yes, I can receive you at my place, I live alone.

- Perfect. For me, Stéphane, it is very important that it is a real moment of sharing beyond the fact that the meeting is priced. I work on the *feeling* and both parties must take pleasure. It is a human exchange. I'm an occasional person, I don't accept many meetings, I let myself go according to my desires and my wishes.

- I am not looking for a professional who is in the mechanism. I need something natural, to spend a pleasant evening without headaches. I am divorced and often on the move. I just want to relax in a jovial and festive atmosphere.

- Great, we are in the same state of mind. Then, to go into the technical details, if I can put it that way, I am rather open, playful. All sex is protected and I don't practice anal, it's not something I like.

- It's not what I want. I am quite classic! I like femininity, I don't have any deviance, softness and good mood will satisfy me!

- Concerning the price, the one-hour appointment is 300 euros including travel expenses, and the additional hour is 200. I don't set the stopwatch to the quarter of an hour, if we take the time to talk over a glass of champagne and it takes forty-five minutes, I'm not going to tell you that I'm leaving in fifteen minutes.

- All this suits me perfectly. When will you be available? How much notice do you need?

26. Negative PCR test

- The day before for the next day, the morning for the evening. In any case, not from one hour to another.

The appointment is given for the next day, Friday, May 15, 2020 at 8 pm, in Caluire.

27. Easier than dating

An hour before leaving, I take a shower and carefully correct my hair removal. I coat my body with oil to make my skin glow and to leave it with a soft, warm monoi perfume. I don't wear any more makeup than usual, the same way I would if I were having a drink with my friends or going shopping. A base of CC Cream, a little sun powder and some ricil. No lipstick or flashy tricks, I like the sobriety and elegance of natural beauty. I dress my legs with a pair of couture stockings that I match with a fine lace bodysuit and a push-up balconette. I hide my lingerie under a skater skirt in black denim, matched with a mao collar blouse opened with three buttons, to let appear the birth of my cleavage. To finish my outfit, I put on suede thigh-high boots of 8 cm square heel and I put on a small perfecto in the same material. The weather is gloomy, I opt for this total black look, a little winter, but I like this outfit, I feel good and can wear it in my everyday life. It is feminine, a bit sexy, just what is needed. It's not vulgar and I don't look like a whore, like the image we can have of girls like me. I simply look like a pretty young woman who has dressed up, to feel attractive. I check that I have gum, my travel toothbrush and condoms in my purse. Unlike Vivian, I don't slip them into my waders, but like her in *Pretty Woman*, I have several kinds. The classic Skin effect for the men who make me want to, the XL version for those that nature has spoiled and the Durex Jeans, plastic feeling, for those that I don't want to feel. And I leave as if I were going to a first Tinder meeting, a few texts and calls beforehand, then a date.

I don't tell anyone, don't leave an address or phone number, I still don't want to bother my girlfriends and get them involved in this. I can't give the responsibility to someone to worry about me and to suffer my choices. I know the risks and I take them, alone. I have no pressure and I am not afraid. I can't imagine anything unpleasant happening to me. I am more concerned about whether I will be able to smoke a cigarette while enjoying my glass of wine or whether this man, who claims to be a sportsman, will be so sporty that he will not tolerate my smoke. I don't know much about him, but I'm so used to this situation that it's become commonplace. And discovery is part of the game. I have the basic ingredients for a great recipe. In the middle of it all, there will be sex and at worst I will have a random time, at best a good evening.

It takes me about thirty minutes to cross Lyon and reach Caluire. The streets are still deserted. We are not allowed to leave our 100 km zone, but we can now drive around without a certificate. I park my car a little away from the indicated address, after having made a tour of the neighborhood and located the meeting place. As always, I am in advance, I observe. Nothing moves, the shutters are closed. It is a small semi-detached house, pale pink. It is not very beautiful, not finished, but aging and gives on the main road. The wall that surrounds it is not plastered, the concrete blocks are bare. I am disappointed, I like beautiful places, it is part of the charm of the meetings. The neighbors are outside in their garden, the children are playing with a plastic rifle shooting at a target while the parents are busy lighting the barbecue. Fond Rose, an annex of Paul Bocuse, just next door, has opened its takeaway. The restaurants are not yet allowed to receive the public, so vehicles come by to pick up their food. This establishment has one of the most pleasant terraces in this sector of Lyon. Only the singing of the birds disturbs the calm of this shady park and the gourmets at the end of their meal, after a few digestives. This is the kind of restaurant that gives the impression of being on vacation at any time of the year. Now it's lifeless and the fledglings have nothing left to peck at at the end of the service.

- I arrived.

- I'll be right there.

I get out of my car and wait in the square. He didn't see my face and I didn't see his. But, as I am alone outside, he can only make the connection. This is always the most awkward moment, like a Kinder Surprise, you don't know what you'll find inside. I'm not apprehensive, I'm in a state of anticipation, so good or bad? Will I have to make a minimum of effort or will the *feeling* be there too?

Two minutes later, a black Range Rover arrives. A pleasant-looking man gets out. His hair is brown and brushed, his eyes are light and his three-day beard is well trimmed. He looks well-groomed and sporty, as he told me during our conversation. He wears jeans, a light blue polo shirt and Nike sneakers. But why

27. Easier than dating

does he arrive in a car? As beautiful and luxurious as it is, I don't like it: "Mathilda? Hello, I am delighted to meet you. I asked you to meet me here because the GPS can't find my address. I live two hundred meters away, do you follow me?"

Our first contact was pleasant. He approached me with a wide smile to kiss me. He has beautiful teeth and it is the only physical criteria I look at in a man, I note this positive point. He looks jovial, friendly and he smells good. The scent of Jean-Paul Gauthier's *Mâle perfumes* my nostrils with a scent that is recognizable among thousands. This familiar smell is reassuring. But, even if from the outside he seems charming, I am a little defensive. Where is he going to take me? I like to locate the places before a meeting. I analyze, it is more reassuring. I'm not facing the wall, I know what I'm getting into before I enter, at least from the outside. And I don't like my car to be seen, I don't like my license plate to be recorded, I always try to keep some kind of anonymity before I know who I'm dealing with. But I have no choice, I'm not going to get in with him or even walk beside him! So I follow him, in my vehicle.

We walk up a small path for less than a minute and arrive in front of a huge wrought iron gate. I see a park behind and notice that there are four mailboxes at the entrance of the domain. There are neighbors, which is a good thing, isolated places are worrying. We drive three hundred meters up through a real green area, past a tennis court and arrive at a gigantic mansion that consists of a first floor and three floors. The façade is pale beige and the pastel blue shutters are openwork with a four-leaf clover on each of them. I count several chimney outlets on both sides of the roof. The place is majestic and magical, less than five minutes from Lyon. I park my car behind his. A *black matte* Maserati is parked a little farther as well as two other vehicles like Mercedes.

- It's beautiful, Stephane, the containment must not have been too difficult here!

- Yes, that's for sure, but the house is divided in four. I only own the top floor. This is my private entrance, it's just me, follow me.

The place is incredible. We take a white stone staircase and climb the three floors that lead to his apartment. I am delighted to be here, I admire, I love to discover this style of house, I love the architecture, the modern, the old, the constructions in general. I feel like a real estate agent or developer, I forget why I'm here and can't wait to enter this place full of history. My disappointment with the small pale pink house is already long gone and the beginning of this appointment fills me with excitement.

- Excuse me, I just got back from the Metropole. Do you know, Mathilda, the hotel Metropole next door?

- Yes, there is a rather nice spa by the way.

- I am a member of their sports club. They just reopened the tennis court, I played a game with a friend, it's more fun than here. Don't blame me if I'm still *fast*, I jumped in the shower so I wouldn't be late for our appointment. For tonight, I've planned a small 2006 Châteauneuf-du-Pape. Unless you prefer champagne? I'm passionate about wine, I have quite a collection. Come on in.

He opens the front door. I enter a large, warm and comfortable living room. The ceiling is French and the beams are meticulously varnished. The floor is covered with a herringbone parquet perfectly waxed giving it a mirror effect. A Roche Bobois

27. Easier than dating

sofa in duck blue velvet sits in the middle of the space and brings the chic side, without being flashy. The kitchen is open to this exceptional living room. It is white, modern and has a central island that serves as a bar and dining table. Three large French windows overlook the Monts d'Or and let in a dazzling light. I take a quick look around to make sure no one else is inside the apartment. The place and the man inspire me confidence, there is little chance that something unpleasant will happen to me tonight. It's probably silly to be reassured by a beautiful house, but luxurious residences are less scary than low-cost housing.

- Wait, come on, if you have two minutes I'll show you my cellar. Do you have two minutes?

- Yes, with pleasure, I love it, I am a true epicurean. Wine and gastronomy are my life!

- Great, we're going to get along great!

We leave the apartment, go down four floors. Fortunately, I am also a sportswoman, because we will have to go back up, and in heels!

- I participate in auctions. I have set up a small space for myself.

- I have already accompanied a friend to buy great wines at Anaf, I found this experience very atypical.

- I know Jean-Claude Anaf very well and I regularly attend his sales.

He opens a small, slightly rickety wooden door that is only secured by a turn of the key. The vaulted room forms an L. The walls are made of golden stone and the floor is covered with large white gravel. Two Chesterfield armchairs are placed at the entrance, accompanied by a coffee table, a bar with four stools and a humidor containing dozens of different varieties of cigars. Around this decor with the appearance of an English private club are carefully lined up, in wooden racks, perhaps ten thousand bottles, each more dusty than the other. I wander among the priceless grands crus and exceptional vintages: Château Margaux, Mouton Rothschild, Montrachet, Cheval Blanc, Petrus, Cristal Roederer, I almost get chills and want to touch them. Where in our daily life we hunt for them, here the dust of each bottle seems to be a gold leaf. He has known me for only five minutes and I can't help thinking that he is crazy or just completely unaware, he is opening his treasure's lair to me. What if I steal it? What if I accept this type of appointment simply with the intention of doing burglaries afterwards? There are sordid stories like this, the young women are used as bait, but in reality there is a whole team behind it. The girl gives her partners in crime the address, the entrance codes and discreetly leaves the door ajar. The evening is then over very quickly, often with a great deal of commotion, but usually with impunity for the criminals.

A man once told me that he found himself naked in the middle of the reception hall at the Novotel Lyon Nord. While he was under the shower, at the beginning of his appointment, the girl took the opportunity to steal everything from him and to leave on the sly. He left the room in pursuit of her without taking the time to get dressed or even to grab a towel. After a run through the hotel corridors, he found himself in Adam's clothes in front of the receptionist, who kindly suggested he call the police. But what do you want to do? Having recourse to this type of service is strictly prohibited. Since 2016, the law "penalization of clients" has come into force. So we now have an official status of "victim"

27. Easier than dating

more glorious, it seems, than "whore". As for our clients, they have to pay a fine of 1,500 euros if they are caught with their hand in the bag or rather with their tail out of their pants. So, informing the police is risking a double penalty and isn't it wiser to tell your wife: "My things were stolen on the train"? But, surprisingly, this misadventure had not scalded him for all that.

I never stole from anyone, even if sometimes I had strong temptations like when one of them, during our first meeting, out of excess of pride or confidence, presented me, before leaving in his dressing room, his watch collection. He opened a simple drawer. With a quick multiplication of rows and rows, I counted twenty-five. The cheapest was the steel Datejust from Rolex. I thought, I must look extremely reliable!

- This is a great place, Stéphane, I love it! Your bottle collection is incredible, exceptional, it makes me dream!

- Yes, you saw! I come here to smoke my cigars, I rest quietly with my friends. I've got everything set up, the lockers, the bar and the temperature is perfect. This is my baby, this cellar. Come on, let's go upstairs and have an aperitif. So Châteauneuf or champagne?

- Châteauneuf ! I am a red wine fan!

We go up quietly, he takes the trouble to wait for me.

- I'm a sportsman, too, so four floors won't scare me. You can go up a little faster, Stéphane!

- Do we do them while running?

- Only if we exchange shoes!

- I see you have a sense of humor!

We enter his apartment again.

- Do you have two minutes, do you want me to show you around? I've been living here alone for eighteen months, I'm divorced. Not all the rooms are furnished, some are a little empty, but come and see.

My time is limited, even if I tend to forget it, he doesn't. You have two minutes, he makes me laugh, of course I have two minutes. On the other hand, it will cost you 10 euros. 300 euros per hour, 5 euros per minute, so 10 euros for two minutes!

We walk down a hallway that leads to three bedrooms, each with its own private bathroom and dressing room. The beds are all *king size* and the decoration is refined. Two of them overlook the park of the domain and the main one overlooks the mountains of Lyonnais. He opens one of the French windows of the living room and invites me to follow him onto the balcony. I am struck by the beauty of the view, stunned, one of the most beautiful I have seen so far in this area of Lyon.

We overlook the Saône and can follow its winding course to Île Barbe. The castle of Collonges, the Auberge de Paul Bocuse and the mountains of the Monts d'Or just in front of us seem to be watching and envying us. My amazed eyes scan the scenery and fix themselves at the bottom of the building. I discover a black bottomed swimming pool hidden under hundred-year-old trees, fifteen or maybe twenty meters long. A few deckchairs and umbrellas surround it as well as a scissor-cut lawn. How beautiful the sunset must be, lying in the middle of this little corner of paradise. I regret not having met him before the confinement, I would have come to take refuge at his place.

- Shall we have a drink, Mathilda?

- Oh yes, with great pleasure!

- You are really beautiful, I am not disappointed at all and you are extremely friendly, natural, smiling, I love it.

- Thank you very much, you too are very charming and I really mean it. It is not to flatter you, I confirm you the "they say", you are very beautiful man.

- I have to tell you, I'm not used to this type of encounter. (They all tell me that!) I was completely against it. Wait, pay to fuck, forgive me for my vulgarity.

- There is no problem. You must not have any difficulty in seducing women, right?

- Yes, but I am very busy with my work. It is a friend who connected me with *escorting*. One day, he told me: "You'll see, you don't take the head, you meet nice people and moreover you win every time! Unlike dating. Because when you invite a woman to a restaurant, give her flowers and pay attention to her, you are never sure of anything. And when you add it all up, it's the same price or even more expensive than an *escort*. My friend is not wrong, it is much simpler and just as pleasant. You know, Mathilda, I'm not looking to remake my life, just to have a good time and break the loneliness of some of my evenings. Like on a dating application I looked for profiles with whom I could get along. I filled in my selection criteria in the algorithm. I still had some bad experiences at the beginning. Well, some bad experiences. When the girl arrives, she sulks, doesn't speak and looks at her watch all the time. She fucks like a robot or a starfish. There is no interest. I also had a young woman who was not at all the same as in the pictures. I was expecting a blonde in her thirties, it was a brunette in her twenties who arrived. I had the impression that these ladies were forced to be there. And I don't want that. Now I'm carefully selecting the profiles. You, your ad is beautiful, your tagline nice and your message clear. I'm glad you're here, I'm having a wonderful time.

- I am also happy to meet you.

- For you too, it must be complicated, it's even worse. You don't know who you'll meet and where you'll end up. I guess you don't like all your clients. Have you ever had bad encounters, had problems?

- I try to select as much as possible, like you. I pay attention to age, the way of speaking, the place of meeting, I don't go to all the areas and make sure to minimize the risks. I have a trustworthy man who knows where I am, how long I have to stay and who is ready to intervene if he doesn't hear from me. And I am armed myself, just in case.

- It's good, you're right, you have to be careful. But don't worry, here you are safe. I won't ask you what you have as a weapon, even if I'm dying to know! But you should know that you won't have to use it, unless you want to hurt me!

It's not true, I don't have a henchman or a gun, but I always place that information during a meeting. It sets the context and maybe, unknowingly, it has already preserved me.

- Does the smoke bother you, Mathilda?

- Absolutely not, I am also a smoker.

- So, feel free to help yourself to my package if you wish.

- Thank you, and the wine is excellent, Stéphane, really.

- It's a little wonder, you're right. Wait, forgive me, I'm failing in all my duties. Here, sorry, I didn't have an envelope.

He extracts from his jeans pocket the 50 euro bills and hands them to me. Automatically, I put them in my handbag, I never count again in front of my host. I prefer this parenthesis to be as stealthy as possible, to avoid any discomfort and that the tariff side does not take too much place in the meeting. It is not in their interest to steal from me. I know their home address or room number. I wait until I leave the premises to check the amount and make sure it's not fake money. I have never had to turn back. However, once, my garage owner informed me that I had given him counterfeit money to pay my repair bill. I didn't notice it and he didn't notice it when he cashed it. It was the bank that alerted him after the money was deposited, and he told me this story during another visit to the garage. Curious to know more about the source of the bills, he took an interest in me.

- But then, miss, what do you do in life?

- I am in the printing business!

He was amused by the joke.

With Stéphane, the atmosphere between us is immediately friendly. He reveals himself naturally, without restraint. After two months of confinement, having met only a few friends, I am delighted by this first evening. To have a social link again, to sip a vintage wine in a sumptuous setting, to exchange and find a semblance of life is a breath of fresh air.

He is originally from Paris and runs an airport in the Rhône-Alpes region. He is proud to tell me that the planes loaded with medical equipment are thanks to him, and I am proud to show him all my knowledge of the aeronautical world.

- Do you want something to eat? You tell me, Mathilda, if you're in a hurry, don't be shy.

- Don't worry, Stephane, I don't do anything out of compulsion. I'd love to have a snack! We've been through such a complicated period that sharing this evening with you is fulfilling.

- Wonderful. I stopped at Mère Brazier, they have reopened the grocery store. Do you like truffles?

- I am a fan of chef Mathieu Viannay and truffles!

- I love you, Mathilda! And really, you are glowing and shining. I'm going to make us a small plate of parma ham with white truffle oil, a drizzle of lemon, a few peppercorns and you're going to taste this wonder! To complete the dish, I'll serve you Mathieu's famous foie gras pie. Perfect, isn't it?

We are sitting face to face on the stools around the island. I've been here for an hour already. The Châteauneuf is almost finished, I'm getting tipsy. He has come up to me three times to steal a little kiss. Quick, shy smacks to express his enthusiasm. We chat amiably, I don't play a role, talk about my life, my professional activities, why and how I came to this type of meeting.

I have never married, have no children, am not here because I am forced or lost, and no one forces me. I have plans, a normal and ordinary life, a family, friends. I simply mix business with pleasure, even if it's a bit of a cliché. The men I meet in my private life often disappoint me. So I chose this way of meeting people. I am never saddened by beautiful promises that lead to nothing. Tonight, the two of us, we expect nothing more than to have a nice time. We don't need to lie to each other, to disguise ourselves behind declarations that are not sincere. Maybe we will meet again, maybe not. But we are willing, clear, we are not playing a game to get what we want from each other. We are very honest, we know how the evening will end and we have accepted the terms of the contract, without perversity or pretence.

I don't play the *escort* who plugs in a stopwatch and invents a character. I am me, only my first name and my phone number are different from those of my everyday life. I like the person

27. Easier than dating

I spend several hours with for the price of one. When I feel good, I don't impose any *timing on* myself, I enjoy the moment, don't work, but have a nice meeting. At some point in the evening, he will want me, and maybe I will too. I will then let him do it.

28. GODDESS OF THE ASS ?

Lyon is a village, we realize that we have friends in common. We could have crossed paths in the establishments we frequent and gone to the same receptions. He opens a second bottle of wine and becomes more and more affectionate and familiar: "My baby, my duck." Now he's calling me names, asking me to go away for the weekend.

- Oh, but you, I adore you! Next week, Mathilda, I'm inviting you to spend the weekend in the Drôme Provençale, in a magnificent farmhouse with a swimming pool, and I'm paying you for it. What do you think of it?

- Why not, let's talk about it later this week.

- Do you have any plans?

- No, but projects and invitations on the first night, I know the enthusiasm that goes down. It's human or maybe male! We'll see if your invitation still stands next week!

He comes up to me, kisses my neck and runs his hand down my legs, showing the bottoms of my stockings. I sit on the high chair, my thighs slightly open, to give him permission to do what he paid me to do. He unbuttons my blouse, languidly licks my nipples, whispering to me how much he loves them. With a delicate hand, he unzips the crotch of my bodysuit and comes gently to affix his tongue and suck my clitoris.

- Oh, Mathilda, I love it so much, you are so good, um, your pussy.

Another one that fits in the statistics! It's incredible how many men spend more time enjoying my vagina than penetrating me. It seems, ladies, that you forbid them this little mouthful in the conjugal bed. It is true that it is an art that few know how to perform. It is often boring, not very exciting, when it is not downright unpleasant. There is the one who waves his tongue like a snake without really knowing what he should lick. The one who sticks his chin and nods his head up and down, rasping your clitoris with his beard. The one who drools on you so much that you feel the moisture dripping down to your buttocks and making a puddle on the sheets. The one who tries to stick his tongue as deep into you as he can, forgetting that he has teeth and that's all you can feel. The one who sucks your lips so hard that you feel like he has a suction cup for a mouth. And the one who understands that a delicate finger is just as important as a bold tongue. When their technique is unpleasant, I tell them. When they are boring, I fake an orgasm. I don't offer the training option in my performances, and when they excel in the art, I selfishly enjoy the moment.

That evening, with Stéphane, I let myself be licked. He is soft, concerned about my pleasure, but I did not enter in a game of seduction with him, then I only want to continue the aperitif and not to start a body to body. But I moan, touch his hair and tighten my thighs against his cheeks to accessorize and make up my lack of excitement. He invites me to follow him into his room and lays me on the bed before continuing what he was doing in the kitchen. I tell him I like it, men want to hear it, they pay me for it. More than their orgasm, they covet mine. They want to feel me vibrate and shiver in their arms. But I don't cum on command and get bored after about ten minutes, and fake orgasm to reward this delicate and affectionate man.

- You are so beautiful, your skin is so soft, Mathilda.

Lying on his back, his sex stretched and perfectly waxed, he burns with desire for me. It's my turn to play with his tongue. His cock is not very long, nor very thick, but circumcised as I prefer them. I throw him a few naughty glances to increase his desire tenfold.

- Do you like my cock, is it good?

- Hmm yes, it is good.

The scene does not last more than three minutes, he does not hold any more and wants to take me. I position myself on all fours in front of him, arch my fleshy rump and, almost instantly, I hear him make his last moan before telling me:

- You fuck divinely well, Mathilda!

I didn't do much though. This reminds me of a question from my friend Chacha:

- Mathilde, are *escorts* goddesses of the ass?

- No, I don't think so! But, the more you *kite*, the better you stand on your board, right?!

I go to the bathroom. Facing the mirror, I feel nothing. I don't feel dirty or soiled. It was rather expeditious and that suits me perfectly. It was like having sex with a boyfriend on a drunken night, with no flavor or performance. I go back to the kitchen, my clothes are on the floor, I get dressed quietly.

After this little intermission, the alcohol vapors have subsided, so he serves us a cocktail based on Japanese Gin ETSU and

Premium Indian tonic. Then a second one. We continue to chat like two friends a little bit drunk for another hour, him hoping to start a new sex game and me sending a text message to my friend Tom: "Hi, my cat, I'm not far from your place. I had a little mission to do, should I stop for a drink?"

After a date, I naturally get on with my life, because it's not a traumatic episode for me. This is my vision of *sex friends*. I can't imagine giving myself away for free without a tomorrow. I decided that if there was no commitment, then I would rather get paid. And so, I am a winner and free. I don't suffer, I don't wait for a call that never comes or only comes late at night, I don't offer myself feeling like I've been screwed twice. Because, unfortunately, I feel that sexual liberation and women's freedom have only tainted our relationships. We have given everything to men and they have used it against us, to get what they want, without caring about our feelings. Because, even if we agree to have sex on the first night, that we have learned not to oppress them, the only thing we hope is that they end up getting attached and committed. But, in this virtual age, where everything is possible with a click, we have become a fruit market. We feel, we taste, we throw away, because on the next stall, the apricot seems sweeter. It seems that men have the same feeling and feel like *sex toys*... Some of them complain about it, they told me! "Mathilda, do you realize that nowadays women have condoms in their handbags, I feel like an object", a customer told me one day. Yes and ? It seems to me that since the dawn of time we manage everything for you. We are your mother, your mistress, your nurse, your secretary, your cook, your cleaning lady, your nanny. If you find that we are starting to take your place, isn't that a positive development for us?

29. I WANT TO WORK FOR YOU

A few days after the deconfinement, on May 25, 2020, I receive by message:

"Hello, I am asking you for a stay that I am organizing from June 9 to 11. We have a villa at two hours from Lyon. We want to spend a nice time between party, barbecue, sex and pool. It's not an orgy, but a real nice time. Are you interested? If yes, what is your price? Greg."

Yesiiii, vacation and party! After these two months of confinement, I can't think of a better mission proposal. *Sea, Sex and Sun*. After a phone call, I go to meet Greg, in his office in his luxury concierge agency in Lyon. I need to know who I'm dealing with, who the men will be and what they want. Going away for three days and two nights is not trivial. I never agree to spend a whole night with someone I don't know. It's too dangerous, anything can happen when you fall asleep. Greg, on the other hand, needs to get to know me. He can't send just anyone, his reputation, security and customer satisfaction are at stake.

He is a nice and handsome man in his thirties. He welcomes me on the terrace of his office, on the top floor of a chic building.

It's 6:30 pm, I'm wearing a summer floral skirt, a crop top and a pair of summer pumps.

- Would you like something to drink? Rosé, fruit juice?

- Rosé is perfect, it's time for an aperitif.

I'm auditioning for a weekend party. I'm not stupid, if I answer Perrier slice, I'm flunked straight away! He opens a bottle of Château Saint-Maur, a classified growth and voted best rosé in the world. I always put ice cubes in my glass of rosé and my taste buds have never been sensitive to the subtleties of this summer wine, but I point out the detail, to flatter him.

- Château Saint-Maur, I see that you are a man of taste.

- I have a feeling that the same is true for you. I'll show you the villa we rented, so you'll know right away where you're going.

He connects to the website Le Collectionist, the ultra luxury version of Airbnb. The house looks sublime, made of white stones with several wings, lost in the middle of the Luberon, between vineyards and mountains. I don't dwell on the pictures, what interests me is to know who the guests are. There are certain personalities from Lyon that I don't want to meet, people for whom I worked in another life, friends of friends or friends from outings to whom I don't talk openly about this aspect of my life.

- As I told you on the phone, the concept of this little weekend is for my clients to let go. They want to party, eat well, drink well and have fun with girls. They're not in the spirit of an orgy, but they want girls, because that's part of the atmosphere. I am looking for five or six *escorts* and they will be three, four, maybe five. They want girls who dance, sing, drink, and participate in the stay, not just sit in the room and wait. It is not even sure that they want sex, but if they do, they must have what they want, when they want it.

They are not robbers, you have nothing to fear. They are all well established in Lyon, it is not in their interest to behave badly. Besides, I will receive you in my offices, that will give you a first guarantee. You know who I am, you have my name, the name of my company. I will also be present during the stay to manage the stewardship. The payment will be done at your departure from Lyon and you will have a driver who will drive you directly to the place and will bring you back home at the end. And if you agree, as we can't go outside the 100 kilometers zone, I will give you a waitress certificate, for a private catering service. That way, we're covered and safe.

- Greg, my participation in this little deconfiguration getaway is basically about the guests. I need you to give me the names. You've already told me the business and I have enough knowledge of the business to know who we're talking about. But there is one person I don't want to meet. I know his wife personally and I wouldn't want to witness or be part of a fine game with her man. If he is there, I won't come. I have nothing to lose, much less than your clients, but I don't like being caught off guard. I want to know what I'm getting into and I'm not willing to do anything for money. If you want, I'll give you my real name, my last name and, in exchange, you'll give me a clear list of the participants. This way we will be *equal* and, if we don't do business, we will know each other that the secret will be well kept.

I learn that the sponsor of this weekend is one of my "idols". I have admired his work for many years, his innovative projects, his transformation of today's world and his vision of tomorrow. I am his first fan, the ambassador of what he does in Lyon. I am always attentive to his news, I don't know him personally and have never had the opportunity to exchange with him or even meet him. The idea that he is present delights me. I think that maybe it's a stroke of fate. No matter how and in what context we meet, I know that I can have a card to play and that this weekend can be an opportunity for work, for contacts, for new projects.

- I agree, Greg.

- Great. Last thing, I'm having trouble recruiting girls. Do you have any girlfriends who might be interested? Do you know any *escorts*?

I don't have any girlfriends in this field anymore, but one of them got in touch with me recently.

"Hello, Mathilda, I am one of your sisters. I am writing to you because I regularly get requests to participate in private parties with small groups of men. Your ad seems to correspond to the expectations of my clients, do you think we can exchange? Kisses, Marie."

I've been with about 15 *escorts in* my life, collaborated with some, just partied with others, even if the difference between the two is thin. But then, is there a typical profile? Do we all have a common point or even several? Maybe we have the nightlife syndrome and the crazy gene. Maybe our male side is a little more developed, I've often heard, "Damn, you've got to have balls to do that."

I always took that remark as a compliment. But I never felt like I was dealing with any particular type of woman. You don't have to be a pirate or a suicide bomber or have been raped or beaten. I've met *escorts* who were also businesswomen, nurses, hairdressers, real estate agents. I have also often met women who wanted to know more, who were attracted by our art and who fantasized about practicing it. This last category is very common: "Mathilde, do you think I can... Would you like to help me to..."

The desire usually remains in the state of fantasy. I have never initiated anyone. I have told my story, talked about my way of proceeding, warned about the pitfalls to avoid, but I have never incited a woman to take the step. It must be a personal process, with a real mature reflection and a deep desire to live love differently, without any trauma or financial pressure.

A few days later, I leave with Greg on Tuesday morning. We have an appointment at 8 am at his office. Finally, he is my driver and we are the first to arrive on the spot. It's a villa at 2 000 euros per night, the place is exceptional, surreal, magical. Greg invites me to relax on a deckchair by the pool while waiting for the guests, but I help him to unload the food for the weekend from the Viano.

- Greg, how many of us will be there during the stay?

- There are eight of us in all. The three clients, you, the three other girls and me. There are eight of us.

- But there are ten cases of Ruinart, fifteen cases of red wine, Aloxe-Corton, Gevrey-Chambertin, as many cases of white wine, rum, whisky. There's all the Cerise et Potiron, Mère Richard's stock and all the charcuterie that Corsica has produced in the last ten years, not to mention the beef ribs, duck breast and other grilled meats. I don't know about you Greg, but I think we're really going to be fair, fair!

I have time to shower, put on a summer floral jumpsuit over my bathing suit and I hear men's voices echoing through the house. I'm nervous. I pace back and forth in my suite. Pressure rarely gets to me, but now I feel like a kid. My heart is racing and

29. I want to work for you

I feel like my voice will be shaking when I say "Hello" for the first time. I have to be natural, I can't arrive with rosy cheeks and say: "Hello Riri, Fifi and Loulou, I'm such a fan of yours and I'm happy to meet you. Hold my resume, I want to work for you, I'm here, but don't just be here."

I blow and go down keeping in mind that they are customers and that, at this moment, when they will greet me, for them, I am only a prostitute.

During my stay, I try to get a job in their companies. I don't hide and I fully assume my way of life, which is not incompatible with a so-called normal job. I am disturbingly honest and sincere, I have nothing to hide. I have learned over time that we are on an equal footing, it is not more honorable to be a man who commands a woman and not less to be this one. They are not perverted predators and I am not a clueless fool. We are anyone and everyone and we don't do anything. Maybe my banker is a prostitute and my insurance company is her client. My universe is rocked by the most banal population, everything is possible, everyone can be part of it, just like this anecdote. One evening I receive a text message:

"Hello, my name is Arnaud, I'm 42 years old, good living. I would like to welcome you to my home in Tassin."

Immediately, it rings a bell, the first name, the age, the city. I compare the number to the one registered in my personal phone book. It's really him! Arnaud, my pharmacist friend. So, my dear, are we bored tonight? Do we want to have some fun? It's a coincidence that he selects my profile, I'm not recognizable on the photos of my ad. It's funny, I was at his place the week before for a dinner with friends. He is not part of my close circle, he is a companion of festive evenings. I never talked to him about this activity, but it probably already came to his ears. Lyon's gossips don't take long to make the rounds. I don't answer his request for services and party at his place a few weeks later. I don't say a word to him, but look at him with a smile: we are in the same boat. I know it, and maybe you do too, but you don't tell me about it, because shh, you can't tell. Let's continue to pretend in society, because I want to be loved by a man who will only see me as a woman and because for you my *escort* status is too taboo to mention.

30. A THOUSAND LIVES

It's December 21, 2020, France has an 8:00 p.m. curfew, and we've just come out of our second lockdown period of the year.

- Where are you in your job search, girl? I know with the year we've had, with Covid it's not easy, but you could use the time we have. I don't know, write a book for example about... a facet of your life. You've always wanted to be a writer, you even ordered a typewriter from Santa Claus when you were 10. I'm sure this is for you, you can become the new Katherine Pancol.

- Or the new Virginie Despentes?

There's a split-second gap. I don't know if she is unaware of my reference or if she knows perfectly well the life of the writer I am talking about. She too went through prostitution before becoming a successful author. Her first novel, *Baise-moi*, was even adapted into a movie. But how does a mother feel about her daughter talking about this? I imagine that the lie, the double life, the impression of not knowing her child and her life is more difficult to take than the facts themselves.

I would like to share this with my mom, it is the only unspoken thing in my life, even though she has suspected it for several years.

I tell her about my "client-friends", my parties, my vacations, but the story is always a little made up. I, on the other hand, am not, and I hope that this is what will remain. I don't talk to her about my manuscript either, which I've been working on for several months now. I'm waiting for it to be finished before I tell him or move on to another project if it doesn't work out.

I am partially unemployed, if I may say so. I haven't isolated myself as I did during the first lockdown, but businessmen are hardly ever on the move again. The heart is no longer in the party, but in the economy. The hotels are almost empty and the business leaders are no longer in the mood to get laid. I'm in the non-essential category. I am the cherry on the cake that you take out when you can already afford to eat one. Lyon is empty, like all the cities in France. It is hidden, sad, lifeless. We are at home, reclusive. There is no more carefree life, except in small groups under the cover of a certificate and a place on the couch so as not to defy the prohibitions in the middle of the night. We who used to cross our metropolis a little bit farted, let's admit it, from now on we fear the controls. The bars are closed, the clubs no longer exist, we no longer meet, no longer exchange. There are no more restaurants, parties, concert halls, social life. For the second time this year, singles are alone at home, in front of their screens *swiping* Tinder profiles and skidding on an *escort* site, because "Fuck" after watching a Youporn, we need flesh, life, sex, real.

I now receive almost exclusively calls and messages from bored men between 25 and 35 years old: "Normally, I go out at parties, I'm pretty good. But right now, well, it's a little *loose*, so I wanted to know if you were available tonight, that we could have a little fun."

242

And almost no men over 55 years old, who make sure not to take any risks. For young men, there is no more going out, no more dating, no more meeting new people. For those who are still on the move, there are no more business dinners, no more *afterwork parties* with colleagues to have fun.

"Young dynamic executive, 32 years old, on the move in Lyon. I am at Globe & Cécile, rue Gasparin. I would like to spend two or three hours with you. What are your conditions and benefits?"

To occupy one's evenings, to find a way to pass the time when only the Uber Eats deliverymen wander in the streets from now on. I am the band-aid of this youth who does not know how to exist anymore. I am the last chance, the hope of a moment of *fun*.

The first confinement had already damaged the couple's relationship, but the second one finished them off. Telecommuting, the need to be with each other constantly, and thus to smother each other, shattered already fragile relationships. Covid has redistributed the cards and given young men the desire to discover the world of paid relationships, attracted by the desire for lightness and freedom. And from now on, I also receive a new kind of demand, a brand new clientele that had never contacted me before:

- Hello, Mathilda, I found your profile on Lovedreams § I am a married woman, I am contacting you, because I would like to offer a night out to my man... Do you meet couples? Do you like the pleasures between girls ? We like to have a naughty night out with three people. We are sweet, respectful, 38 and 39 years old, pleasant physical, in Lyon. If it is possible, I let you answer me § thank you and see you soon ! Alice.

- Hello, Alice. What a lucky man he is! I hope he knows it. Unfortunately, I am not attracted to women. I can indulge in caresses and kisses, but I do not practice female oral pleasure. Yours sincerely.

- Ah, ah mercii § I think he knows, yes! Thanks for your answer. We'll discuss this fantasy again. If it turns out to be an evening for two rather than three, I'll let you know again, have a nice day.

This is not an isolated case, I go from zero requests to one every week. The closing of the libertine clubs has a lot to do with it. They are always women who approach me, they are nice, they put *smileys* in their messages, they propose me to participate in private libertine evenings, in naughty aperitifs between couples. Even if I don't answer favorably, I like to receive this kind of request, I find that it brings a little freshness. I like to know that the world still turns, that people live, that there are somewhere, around me, people inclined to thwart the rules that society imposes on us. I am not for the moment willing to discover the libertarianism environment, neither for work nor in my private life, even if I have already tested threesomes, in its two forms, even if I am what can be qualified as a "liberated" woman. Libertarianism, in the first sense of the term, which is practiced in couple is a different approach of sexuality. I don't believe in eternal fidelity, even if I also fantasize about it. I am convinced that libertines are happier than other couples. The possession of the body is not a guarantee of love. But, my mind is too narrow to accept to see my partner in the arms of another. My mind probably has nothing to do with it. It is certainly a matter of trust in oneself and in the other. But who is the other for me? What is the balance of my heart after two more years of celibacy and prostitution? I have told the story of my life as an *escort*, the luxury hotels, the men who supposedly worship me, the vintage wines, the orgasms, the fantasies and the envelopes; the crazy weekends where I am paid to party, the clients who are my friends, even my lovers. Even if, in most cases, I'm just a disposable consumer product, I've still managed to turn a few trials into something more than just tickets and more than just a girl who gets paid.

"Hi, Mathilda, how are you? I'm having a dinner party at my house, I'd love you to meet my son, my daughter-in-law and my ex-wife! There will be Chateauneuf and truffles! Are you coming?" Since leaving the first lockdown, Stéphane and I have been sending each other messages and photos of our vacations. I've given him my personal phone number, he's given me his membership at the Metropole so I can go sunbathing by the pool in the summer and has introduced me to some of his friends. I'm his big buddy," he tells them.

- But are you screwing her?

- But no, Mathilda is my friend, I love her.

- But how did you meet?

- At a party, at the restaurant La Maison, in Gerland.

We have become close and it is not always about money or sex. Our relationship is healthy, frank and without any history. He still has a little trouble calling me Mathilde, but I am used to being called Mathilda. Sometimes I think for a few fractions of a second, I juggle my two identities, I go from one to the other, to the point of forgetting what my name is.

I always have a plan, a friend, an acquaintance, a client. I get the best table with a view of Lyon at the last minute in a starred restaurant, invitations to previews, seats in dressing rooms, free helicopter rides, access to underground restaurants, privileges on this and that, discounts in any area. I often hear my girlfriends say:

"Without Mathilde, we would never have done this."

"Only with Mathilde can something like this happen to us."

"Normally, I don't get along with girls, but you, Mathilde, I adore you."

"I would so like to have your life, Mathilde, you're right."

But between us, if I break Mathilda's chip, what do I have left? The men who don't pay me don't even realize that others do, that for me it is a privilege to offer them a free service that I normally charge for.

At the time, as part of my YouTube channel, I approached a cooking prodigy to propose a collaboration. We met, liked and desired each other. We fell in love, once in his lab and a second time in Montreux, Switzerland, where I joined him during one of his trips. Then I stopped responding to his solicitations. He doesn't have anything to offer me other than some sex, I don't need it. Very regularly, he sends me a "want" message. No "hello" or "how are you", just "want", sometimes even with a picture or video of his private parts. He waits for me to meet him between two of his professional appointments, so that he can get out of here in a hurry. He doesn't even realize that he is behaving much worse than my clients.

- Mathilde, when do we meet?

- When you have at least one night to devote to me and take care of me.

- I don't have time, I have too many things to deal with.

- And I'm better than a dick on your counter.

Nevertheless, for more than a year, he continues to send me "envy". I think that I am part of his *list of* "groupies" and that his diffusion is massive until I get one: "I'm coming".

Then there was this Sétois, expatriate in London, who contacted me via Instagram. The magic of social networks! "I have box seats for the *Champions league* game tonight, do you fancy going with me?"

I'm not interested in soccer, even if : "If you don't jump, you're not from Lyon". And then, I prefer the atmosphere of the south wing to the one of the small fours. Singing and drinking beer is what I enjoy at the stadium. But I also have a lot of fun in the unlikely situations, in the unexpected, which usually result in unforgettable moments. We've all experienced this: "Tonight, I'm not going out". Then you get motivated and have the best night of your life. Maybe that's the day you met your husband. I'm sitting on my couch, my hair is a mess, I have nothing to lose and who is it, maybe it's fate striking again. If he had said to me, "Marry me," I would have said yes. But instead he told me, "You're too *full on*, don't expect anything from me."

It's true, I'm always into everything. For a moment, and like a bellows, it falls back.

Then there was Thibaut who, the first morning he woke up at my place, went to buy breakfast. So cute. But he came back with a full bag of groceries, his brand of tea, his flavor of jam, a kilo of cane sugar in pieces, a liter of olive oil, a butter plate, a filet of potatoes, eggs, steaks. When he said to me: "I am living the most beautiful love story of my life", it finished me. It finished me off because I am full of contradictions with men. I play hide and seek with myself. When something serious is going on, I run

30. A thousand lives

away. My life as an *escort* doesn't allow me to consider a relationship, we always start with a lie: "What do you do in life?" For one, I am a *broker* in aviation, for the other in charge of business development of a music studio or unemployed, because since the Covid I lost my job in the event industry.

"Even if for everything there is a part of truth, forgive me if I lied to you, if I too did not call you back, if I did not agree to see you again and at the time you did not understand why, as I certainly told you, all this has nothing to do with you, I am just not ready, for now."

I have had a thousand lives, a thousand jobs, a thousand lovers. I'm proud of my journey, of who I am even if I haven't accomplished anything yet, but I've managed to blossom, to get up every morning telling myself that life is beautiful and to go to bed every night thanking the person or persons who give me the strength to be better than the day before. I think that if there is a final judgment, our qualities of heart will prevail over our way of life. Our existence cannot be reduced to our relationship with sex or what is on our plate. I think it would be an offense to our creator to reduce his intelligence to such percepts. Doesn't our soul dissociate from our body before joining the heavens? Sometimes I talk to my dad during my prayers. I'm not sure if he gets a good laugh out of it, but I imagine he's even more surprised to see me praying. And frankly, it's nothing to get excited about. I don't like that anyway, drama, dramatic comedies, stories that end badly. If I take everything lightly, it is to limit the problematic situations. But, be careful, I am not an anarchist, I am a libertarian.

Since the end of the first confinement, I don't smoke pot anymore, THC scotches me, isolates me, I don't feel like doing anything, I see life in black, and maybe I'm finally becoming an adult! A few hits on a joint of grass from time to time in the evening with my girlfriends, and still. I even quit smoking three months ago, for how long?... I'm afraid of getting fat, of course, it even haunts me, but I drink herbal tea and vapourize a little. I sometimes open a bottle of wine, alone, at home, sometimes even two. But if one day life takes its course, I will probably not have a loyalty card at my wine shop anymore. In the meantime, I try not to become an alcoholic, I never have a stock at home. A new addiction can happen so fast, as fast as time goes by. 2021 has come and gone. Happy New Year! In four months I turn 37, and while I'm always optimistic, I'm pretty realistic. My biological clock is telling me to get off my butt if I ever want to be a mom, even though I never wanted to and still don't. Commitment with no way back, that scares me. And I think I am also free not to want children without society having anything to say about it. But, a beautiful love story to vibrate, the idea starts to appeal to me again. Updating my CV makes me realize that I have undertaken a lot of projects without ever really completing one. I'm always throwing myself into improbable, unattainable challenges, my loved ones constantly supporting me because, "There's no way this will work, but if it's you, maybe there's a chance."

I have a BEP in sales, but none of the bosses I've worked for knew about this. I have a bachelor's degree, a bachelor's degree, I have what they require on the ad. If I think I can do it, then I can do it. And I do it. In the end, all these expressions are not so "stupid"! Four months ago, the Word document I'm currently writing on had a character count of zero. 66,669 words later, I'm typing away on my MacBook, sitting at the desk I've set up in my apartment. I remember being 12 years old, locked in my teenage bedroom, typing on my typewriter: *Mortiferous*. Chapter 1 begins:

"I stay for hours contemplating the outside world around me. Person after person, thing after thing. I wonder what the true meaning of their lives is. And especially what is the true meaning of my life. I don't know everything, but I feel like I know every-thing and have seen everything. I feel like a rebel and at the same time I am afraid of the future.

Twenty pages and eight chapters later, my first book ends:

"But you, if you hear sweet music, if you see a bright light. If you feel that you are being pushed towards a better life, if you are afraid and this world horrifies you. Then don't think about anything else, but don't forget that you are the master of your destiny."

This *bestseller*, full of surreal questions for a 12 year old, was published in ten copies at Copie + and distributed to the VIP members of my family clan. I think I have in my library the only edition that has survived time.

But, then, was I predestined to become an *escort*? Is it my professional background? My education? The men who shared my life ? My disappointments in love ? My girlfriends ? The people I've known, the environment I've evolved in? My love for the opposite sex or just for sex ? My thirst for freedom and adventure? What really led me to this art? But do we really need to find symptoms that would explain why I am me? Because, finally, I am nothing else but that. So, can I be stopped?

- Hello Mathilde, this little message to know if you are well. I hope that sport keeps you in shape. I haven't forgotten you!

This is a troubled and complex time. I'm navigating by sight and for the moment the projection is more about dismissal than about hiring. But, I keep you in a corner of my mind and, if I have a job opportunity, I think of you, I promise you. Love to you, see you soon.

 - Hello Loulou, thank you for your message. I know it's not easy right now. And I know for sure that you will help me the day you can. By the way, maybe you have some contacts in the publishing world. I've written a manuscript and would like to get it published. I look forward to talking with you. Love to you and love to Rifi and Fifi for me.

31. At the end of my dreams

Wednesday, October 20, 2021, almost a year has passed. In a few days, this manuscript will go to the printer and it will soon be in bookstores. I am making the final corrections, learning this new exercise, this new profession of being an author. I spend an average of twelve hours a day on my computer. I read, write, rewrite, think, smoke, smoke again, yes, I have taken up smoking. Am I not making a mistake by putting my entire story on paper? I think it's fabulous to have succeeded for once in seeing a project through to the end and to have, thanks to the strength of my work and my perseverance, been able to find a publisher, without anyone recommending me or helping me. But, am I not making a mistake by imagining that society is ready to hear that I am free of my body and that I love this life? All the people I met and to whom I revealed my art reacted in such a positive way that I started writing this book, because it is true that this universe intrigues and fascinates, and that too few positive testimonies are given.

- Elise, we do more than just ride together. Now we are friends. I have to tell you something, because in a few months it won't be a secret. I am an *escort*.

- Oh yeah? It's a dating method that has often attracted me, and even more so when I feel that my guy treats me like his bitch.

***

- Hello, my name is Arnaud, I am 42 years old, good living. I would like to welcome you at my home in Tassin.

- Hello, Arnaud, I hope that your stay in Corsica went well and that you are managing with the hazards of the pharmacy!

- But we know each other, who are you?

- Indeed, we know each other and I am in a teasing mood today. That's why I'm replying to your message, which is not the first one you've sent me!

- If you feel like revealing yourself, drop by for lunch, you know the address, right?

- By heart!

Arnaud can't be shocked by this announcement and he tells me that he never had any suspicion about me, but confides to me that several of his friends are *escorts*. Normal and ordinary people, we are.

- My little mother, I have something to tell you. You know, at Christmas almost a year ago, you suggested to me that I write a book. At that time, I didn't tell you about it, because the project was still in progress. But now it's finished and I have to sign my publishing contract.

- That's great, girl, why don't you look excited?

- Because I won't do it without your approval, my little mommy, and without you having read it. Remember the author I told you about, Virginie Despentes, do you know her?

- But, girl, your old mother is no fool and I'll tell you something. I may not have many morals, but I'm not shocked at all. You play with your charms, I've known it for a long time, a mother knows her children. And the important thing, my daughter, is that you are happy, that no one hurts you and that at the same time you realize yourself. This book is the first project that seems viable to me, so don't question yourself and you can always come and live with your mother if things don't work out as you hope.

- Aren't you afraid of people's eyes?

- People always have something to say, girl. And I'm proud of you, writing a book, can you believe it? You're making my dream come true.

- So, write, my little mummy, I can track you!

***

- Marina, I am an *escort*.

- Sister, I'm so relieved that you're finally opening up. You know, Mom and I have often wondered about you, and we were afraid that you might have gotten involved in some kind of trafficking. *Escorting is* not a conventional job, but you are not hurting anyone. And if we're honest, we're all someone's bitch, our husband's, our boss's or even the state's. Isn't it said that the state is the biggest pimp of all?

***

- Hello, Mathilde, I'm writing this email on a personal basis. I am part of a reading committee to which you sent your manuscript. I wanted to tell you that in ten years of career, your book is my second favorite. For a long time, I have wanted to discover your universe and I am very attracted by this way of meeting. Do you think we can call each other to discuss it?

- On the condition that you tell me which publisher you work for!

***

- Mathilde, congratulations. I loved your book, I'm sure it will work.

- Thank you, Will. You know how much I hold you in my heart and I really need you to be honest with me, I feel like I am playing so big.

- As I told you before, out of ten women, there are five who fantasize about it, two who have already done it and three who have an overly selective relationship with their body! Go for it, baby.

***

- My Mathilde, you can be proud of yourself and I am. I could even testify if you want.

- Thank you my Steph, we celebrate this news with a Chateauneuf and truffle?

***

- I put the copy of your manuscript you gave me to read in the safe.

- Next to the ingots? I am honored, Loulou! But I'm so afraid of what's going to happen with this book.

- It's okay to be afraid, all entrepreneurs are afraid. But you don't care, you're right and I'm sure there are many of us who think so. In a few years, when we talk about this again, the version I keep will be a *collector's* item. You know that Riri and Fifi can't wait to read it, it's not for everyone to be in a book!

***

- My Benoit, you know how much you mean to me, how much I love you. We have known each other for seven years now and you have been waiting for three years for me to say "yes" to your proposal of marriage.

- I remember perfectly your rhetoric, you were the first woman to turn me down: "Don't expect anything from me, I can't promise you that you are the only one", you told me.

- That's why you don't defuse the story! I can't promise you that you are the only one, because my life doesn't allow me to, I am an *escort*, my Benoit.

- You will always surprise me my darling, and you know very well that with me you will be the happiest of women. I will wait again and, the more the years pass, the more I have my chances!

So, since all the people I love love me, I'm going to put my name on the bottom of the publishing contract. I feel like I'm on the edge of the bridge again, facing the void, I jump, but this time I know all my friends and family will be there at the reception.

"What's the use of being famous without deserving it, I've always got the truth hanging from my lips, And the past follows

31. At the end of my dreams

me day and night, I don't know in what state I'll get to the end of my dreams, I've got a strong heart, I've got my hands full, When they're empty, will you tell me that you love me?"[8]

8. Booba, *Au bout de mes rêves*.

Acknowledgements

"Forget that you don't have a chance. Go for it!" It was with this mindset that I began writing this book.

Thank you to Clémence, Charlotte, Eddy, Sophie, Anthony, Yohann, Élisa, Émi, Amel, H. B., Yaya, Jack, Xavier, Franck, Adeline and my girlfriends' girlfriends, who supported me and who formed my first reading committee. I am incredibly lucky to have you as friends.

Thank you to my clients who encouraged me and volunteered to read before publication. You have helped me grow and made my quest for freedom possible.

Thank you to my colleagues who, in my moments of doubt, gave me the strength to not give up, for them and for all TDS. We each have our own personal story, but a common motto: "We exist".

Thanks to my editor who knew how to adapt to my personality, I couldn't have had a better "partner" to serenely lead this publication.

Thank you to my sister, my double opposite and yet so identical.

And above all, thank you to my mom, the best, and everyone says so! Thank you mamounette for believing in me since always, for letting me evolve without trying to change me and for accepting my life, because a world without differences is a rainbow without colors.

I love you.

TABLE OF CONTENTS

Table of contents

Best sellers Max Milo Editions

Hitler's banker, Jean-François Bouchard

Confessions of a forger, Éric Piedoie Le Tiec

The Koran and the flesh, Ludovic-Mohamed Zahed

Governing by fake news, Jacques Baud

Governing by chaos, Collectif

A political history of food, Paul Ariès

Mad in U.S.A.: The ravages of the "American model",
Michel Desmurget

Mondial soccer club geopolitics, Kévin Veyssière

Putin: Game master?, Jacques Braud

Treatise on the three impostors: Moses, Jesus, Muhammad,
The Spirit of Spinoza

TV Lobotomy, Michel Desmurget